A Funny Thing about TEACHING

Connecting with Kids Through Laughter...and Other Pointers for New Teachers

Jack Rightmyer

Cottonwood Press, Inc.

Fort Collins, Colorado

Requests for permission should be addressed to:

Cottonwood Press, Inc.
109-B Cameron Drive
Fort Collins, Colorado 80525

E-mail: cottonwood@cottonwoodpress.com
Web: www.cottonwoodpress.com
Phone: 1-800-864-4297
Fax: 970-204-0761

ISBN 978-1-877673-78-8

Printed in the United States of America

To Judy, who keeps me laughing in good times and in bad

Table of Contents

Don't Smile Until Christmas......................................11

Classrooms of Darkness 21

Classrooms of Light 35

Finding My Way..45

What Makes a Good Teacher?.................................49

Learning to Laugh 53

Choose Your Attitude 65

Being Playful..71

Being Playful Can Lead to Success 87

Nothing Funny About Discipline 99

Forgiving and Forgetting 113

Building Strong Relationships 119

Smiles on the Last Day 129

Appendix 133

A Unit on Humor 135

Acknowledgments

Getting a book published has been a lifelong dream for me. Well, I really wanted to play second base for the Boston Red Sox, and then I wanted to be an Olympic marathon runner, but when these goals didn't work, I moved on to my next goal—to get a book published. It only took me twenty years to accomplish this goal.

I want to thank Cheri Thurston for publishing this book and helping make it the best book I could write. I would also like to thank all the wonderful teachers and coaches who have taught me through the years, and all the teachers I've worked with out in the trenches of education day after day, year after year.

"Whether you think you can, or can't, you are usually right."
– Henry Ford

Thanks to Joel Goodman at the Humor Project for giving me the opportunity to spend my sabbatical learning about the benefits of humor.

Thanks to the *Daily Gazette* for giving me the chance to interview some of the best writers in the world, and thanks to William Kennedy for creating the New York State Writers Institute, which has brought these great writers to Albany, New York.

Thanks to my wife Judy and my two children, Erin and Paul, who bring humor and love to me every day, and thanks to my mom and dad who always bought a book for me even when they couldn't afford it.

A Funny Thing About

Don't **SMILE** Until Christmas

It was my first day as a teacher. I was 22 years old, only a few months out of college, and I had a brand new briefcase and two ties. I would wear one tie on Mondays, Wednesdays and Fridays, and the other on Tuesdays and Thursdays. I had spent most of the weekend going over my five-day lesson plan, and I had almost memorized my schedule for each day of the week. "It's important to get off to a good start," my cooperating teacher had told me the previous fall when I was student teaching.

I might have seemed prepared, but I was really scared out of my mind. What made this day even more agonizing was that I was teaching at my high school alma mater, where I had graduated only four years before. I was now working with the teachers who had once taught me. The pressure was on.

At that time, I was still living with my parents, so in many ways I felt like a high school student myself, not a high school English teacher. "You look very handsome," my mother said as she kissed me goodbye. She straightened my Monday-Wednesday-Friday tie.

"This isn't any old summer job," my dad said. "This is a career. You'd better take it seriously."

I nodded my head and walked to my car, carrying the brand new black briefcase.

The 20-minute drive to school seemed to take forever. I felt like a dead man walking to his execution. My hands were shaking, my stomach was turning, and I knew I could very easily throw up in the car all over my clothes and brand new black briefcase.

When I arrived at school many students were waiting around in the front foyer. I felt as if they were all laughing and pointing at me as I walked by them and down the hall to the main office. After a

> *"We rarely succeed at anything unless we have fun doing it."*
> – John Naus

quick stop to check my mailbox, I moved through the hall to my homeroom. "Good luck, Jack," one of the teachers said. "You'll do great," another teacher said.

I tried to smile, and I waved to acknowledge their words of encouragement, but my brain was having a hard time getting the rest of my body to cooperate. My hand was so shaky I could barely open the classroom door. And then, finally, I was in.

The classroom looked pretty sparse. I had put up a few posters that some teachers had given me the week before, but they were mostly dull posters, freebies given away by publishing companies. They were basically advertisements to get teachers to buy that company's anthology, but still, they took up some space on the blank walls.

When the bell rang, the halls were immediately congested with high school students, mostly big and hairy looking, at least to me. I stood for a few minutes in the hallway by my door—wasn't that what a teacher was supposed to do? It seemed as though everyone was looking at me.

"Hi, Mr. Rightmyer," a student at a locker near my room said.

"Hi," I said, trying to sound like an adult.

I was amazed that he knew my name already. In fact, everyone entering my homeroom seemed to know my name. It was a strange feeling. I guessed I had been a big topic of discussion over the summer. Students must have been telling their parents that a new teacher, a Mr. Rightmyer, had been hired to teach tenth and twelfth grade English. In fact, this Mr. Rightmyer had even graduated from this same high school only four years before.

What I found out a few days later was that everyone knew my name because it was printed above my classroom door.

When homeroom ended, I walked upstairs to the faculty room. That year, the first two periods of the day were free periods for me, so there I sat in the faculty room, pretending to look busy and feeling very uncomfortable around many of the teachers who had once taught me. I kept calling them "Mr." or "Mrs.," and they kept trying to get me to call them by their first names. Everyone was throwing out free advice for me.

"You've got to come down hard," one teacher said.

"You're young. Don't let them take advantage of you," another said.

"Don't smile until Christmas," a third said, "because if you do, you've lost them."

The chaplain of the school could only smile and shake his head.

"I've been praying for you all weekend," he said.

I sat there studying my seating plans, memorizing my lesson plans, and practicing looking and sounding mean. I hadn't even met my classes yet, and already I didn't trust them. I didn't even like them. If what these teachers were telling me was true, these kids were out to get me, and I wasn't about to let that happen. As my dad had said, this wasn't any old summer job, this was a career, and I had to get off to a good start.

And that meant I couldn't smile till Christmas.

Starting out tough. When it was finally time for me to teach my first class, I was ready. I marched down that hallway, practically ordering students out of my way. There was no way they were going to take advantage of me. I made sure not to smile at anyone.

A few students were gathered at my door. They said "hello," and I nodded at them but didn't smile. A few of the students were brothers and sisters of friends I had gone to school with. They were trying to act like they were friends of mine, but I wasn't going for it. One of them, the brother of one of my best friends, asked how my day was going. "Sit down," I told him.

Very quickly, I introduced myself. I told them I had been a recent graduate of their high school. One student in the back yelled out, "You and my brother got drunk at his high school graduation party." The entire class laughed.

"Don't ever speak out again," I snapped at him. "Raise your hand and wait to be called on."

The class quickly settled down. A few students were exchanging looks. "He's a mean guy," they were probably thinking. "We had better not take advantage of him."

I kept that demeanor for the rest of the day. All business! No smiles!

As I was leaving to go home, Paul O'Brien, the chairman of the English department, stopped in to see me. "How did everything go?" he smiled.

It was a relief to see him. I could finally smile. "It went great," I said. "They did everything I asked them to do."

He laughed. "That won't happen every day," he said.

We talked a bit on the way down the hall, but what I remember the most was what happened as we passed students. Every one of them spoke to Paul. They all seemed happy to see him, and he seemed happy to see them. He joked around quite a bit with the students, and it felt nice to be in his company.

When he opened the door to his room, my eyes must have bugged out. It didn't look like a classroom. He had a couple of old rocking chairs, a rug, a reading lamp in one corner. His posters weren't from textbook companies. They were of rock stars and movies. "I'm not sure if the Woody Allen poster belongs here or by the door," he asked.

"By the door," I said and then asked if I could sit in one of his rocking chairs. He had wooden bookshelves, and there was a radio and a record player in the back of the room. I felt like I had entered one of my friend's dorm rooms from college. "I love how you set up your room," I said.

"I like to have it feel like home," Paul said. "My wife always comes in just before the school year begins and helps decorate with me."

"I'll bet your students love to come in here."

Paul smiled. "I think so. Anyway, I like it."

I helped him move the poster. There were numerous posters on the chalkboard, and he only had a little room left for notes. "You don't have much room to write on the board," I said.

"I don't use the board a lot," he said. "I try to keep the class active. I keep the class very hands-on."

"My room doesn't look anything like this," I said.

Paul smiled. "It'll take you a few years to find your style, and to find how you want to decorate your room."

On our walk down the hall and out the door to our cars, Paul said, "You're going to learn a lot this year. You're going to make many mistakes, and you'll learn from them. It'll be at least three years before you really start finding your own teaching style."

I drove home thinking that three years is such a long time.

Being all business. For the next few months, I continued my strategy of being all business in the classroom. I found that my classes would quiet down if I had a board full of notes when they walked in. "Sit down," I would bark at them, "and copy down the notes. Let's go. We don't have all day."

This seemed to work for a while, but after a few weeks I started to get some mini-rebellions. "I don't have a pen," one student would say.

"I can't write today because I hurt my hand," another would say.

There always seemed to be grumbling, and I kept hearing a lot of muttering about how boring the class was. "You're the ones who are boring," I wanted to say. "I never acted like you when I went to this school."

I suffered like that through much of the fall, trying desperately to keep up with my paper correcting, to keep busy so I didn't have to admit how miserable I was. My parents had spent all this money on my bachelor's degree so I could get a decent job, and I hated it. It wasn't any fun. I wasn't sure I would even be able to finish out the school year.

My misery continues. The low point came in early November when Paul O'Brien came in for his first teacher observation. We were reading *Huckleberry Finn*, and the class was hating it. I had planned what I thought was a good lesson, but I needed some feedback from the students. I wanted them to get into groups and answer questions about how they had faced prejudice. I thought this would be a great way to begin our discussion of slavery.

I moved them into groups and right away they were all complaining. "I want to be with Mary," one girl said.

"We don't want him in our group," another boy at the opposite end of the room said.

"My chair is too small."

"There's gum on this desk."

I just kept running around the room putting out fires, trying not to rant and rave, and definitely feeling that I had lost control. It was the longest 45 minutes of my life.

Paul just sat in the back of the room smiling and writing in his notebook. At the end of the class, as he was walking down the aisle, I heard a student ask him if he could take over and be our teacher. "You already have a good teacher," Paul said, and then he smiled at me and said, "Tomorrow after school, let's sit down and go over this evaluation. Stop by my room."

I said I would stop by, thanked him for coming in, and decided I would begin looking that night for a job at McDonald's or Pizza Hut. It was quite obvious there was no way I was ready to be a teacher yet.

That night I wanted to be honest and tell my parents that I had tried, but I just wasn't cut out to be a teacher. But they were just so proud of me. I couldn't bear to tell them what was really going on.

It was a bit hard getting to sleep that night. The next morning, on my drive to work, when I was stopped at a red light, I glanced over to my left and saw some construction workers setting up cones. What a wonderful job, I thought, to be outside most of the day, to not be interrupted by nasty high school kids, to work with your hands, and when you were done, to go home and not have to do anything job-related. After work, construction workers could just watch TV, play music, or read a book or magazine. They didn't have to correct any papers or write any lesson plans. And they probably got paid more than the average teacher.

My first evaluation. When I stopped by Paul's room the next day, he was listening to a Robert Klein comedy album about going to the dentist. It was hilarious, and we both laughed. After a few minutes, Paul stopped the recording, wiped his eyes and said with a big smile, "My study hall has been so noisy lately that I can't even read, so I told them that tomorrow if they're quiet for the first 20 minutes, I'll play Robert Klein for the last ten minutes." He motioned for me to take a seat near his rocking chair.

I had been nervous when I entered his room, but after listening to the comedy album, I relaxed a bit. "I was up late looking through the newspaper for any job openings at McDonald's or Pizza Hut," I said, sitting down.

Paul laughed. "Now why would you want to look for work there?"

"The class you came in to observe was chaos," I said. "The kids were so noisy. I'm sure it was horrible to watch."

He sat down and leaned back in his rocking chair, holding his notes from the observation. "I think you did a great job," he said.

Maybe he was getting me confused with another teacher, I thought. "My plan about the grouping didn't seem to work out," I said.

"The kids were off task a bit," he said, "and they were a bit noisy, but I was watching you, and I saw some good things."

Maybe he's saying all this because he's going to fire me and he doesn't want me to feel so bad, I thought. "We only got about halfway through my lesson plan," I said. "The kids weren't focused at all."

And then he began talking about all the positives he saw. "I like how you were willing to try something risky, like having a discussion about prejudice," he said. "I like how you were trying to get the kids to talk about when they've felt prejudice in their lives. That's a great way to get kids to connect with a story or a character. And you've got a good presence in the room. You just need to be yourself more, and that comes with time and experience."

"But what about all that noise?" I asked.

"When you start being yourself more, that noise will settle down," he said.

He then encouraged me to sit in on a few of his classes. "Come in whenever you feel like it. If you want to watch only the beginning of class, that's fine. Or just come in at the end."

And periodically throughout the year, that's what I would do. Watching Paul run a class discussion was better than watching a favorite TV show. He was a performer, sometimes reading from the text, sometimes letting students read, but always full of life and fun. Kids showed up on time for Paul's class. They wanted to sit up front and raise their hands. They were active students who felt comfortable taking risks.

And there was always the sound of laughter. No matter what the book or lesson was, Paul could always find something funny to say or do. He would play recordings of comedians or show parts of funny movies and always relate them to his lesson for the day. Kids were having so much fun, they didn't realize they were learning, and I was having so much fun, I didn't realize I was learning how to teach.

After a few weeks of observing Paul, I could feel my own teaching style gradually begin to change. I even accidentally smiled a few times while I was teaching, long before Christmas vacation. On the way to school, I stopped looking for construction workers and fantasizing about their work.

Maybe this teaching gig might pay off after all, I thought.

Classrooms of **DARKNESS**

I know that I would not have lasted very long in the classroom if I had not found a mentor in Paul O'Brien. There was no way I was going to stay in a profession that wasn't any fun. I don't need a large paycheck, but I do need a purpose for waking up early in the morning and getting out of that warm bed. Paul showed me it *is* possible to have a great time teaching and to have his students have just as much fun.

"A person without a sense of humor is like a wagon without springs–jolted by every pebble in the road."

– Henry Ward Beecher

Insecurity, insecurity. One reason I did not enjoy myself in the beginning is that I had absolutely no confidence as a teacher. I was tense and nervous.

I felt more like a prison guard than a high school English teacher. My students did not respect me. All I did was bark at them, which is certainly not the best way to create a positive relationship.

Part of my insecurity as a first-year teacher had to do with my age. I was 22 years old and teaching high school seniors who were sometimes only four or five years younger than me. While I was learning how to pace a 45-minute classroom lesson, I was also learning the subject matter, usually the night before I was teaching it. Although I had received decent grades in college, I suddenly saw that there was an awful lot I didn't know. And my students kept asking so many tough questions.

"What's the difference between *effect* and *affect*?"

"Is *a lot* ever spelled as one word?"

"Was Mark Twain a racist?"

It's no wonder I didn't walk in every day relaxed and ready to start cracking a few jokes with my students, as Paul O'Brien did.

However, an advantage I had was that I also was the coach for our school's cross-country team. Even if I had a horribly unhappy day in the classroom, I still had from 3:00 p.m. until 5:00 p.m. every afternoon to run with my team, relax, and laugh.

One day, one of my runners, who was also in my tenth grade English class, said to me, "Mr. Rightmyer, you're so much fun at practice. How come you're not fun like this in class?"

I felt hurt, but inside I knew he was right. I *wasn't* "fun" in class. At the time, I thought I was supposed to be serious when I was teaching. As my father often reminded me, "This is a real job." I didn't think you were supposed to laugh and have fun at a real job.

Coaching was different. It was supposed to be fun, and I had over 40 kids on the team who wanted to be there. They didn't complain and roll their eyes when I told them the workout. I was relaxed as a coach. My enjoyment was coming through, and I was able to connect very well with the runners.

One reason I was so relaxed was my confidence level. I had been a runner all four years of high school and for four more years at a Division I college program. I knew what I was doing. I didn't have to stay up late learning what I was going to coach.

What I needed in the classroom was the same confidence. As I struggled to find my way, I started thinking about teachers who had made an impression on me over the years, either positively or negatively.

One person who immediately came to mind was Brother Mooney.

A trip to the dark side. The first time I ever saw Brother Mooney was when I was an eighth grader visiting the Catholic high school I would be attending in September. It was an exciting day for me to visit with a few of my eighth grade friends.

The principal gave each of us a schedule to follow for the day. We attended eleventh and twelfth grade classes, and the regular kids in those classes pretty much ignored us until we went to the chemistry lab, where I teamed up with two long-haired students who seemed more intent on setting things on fire than in following the directions for the experiment.

"What's your name, squirt?" asked one of the students with long blond hair.

I told him my name.

"Why do you want to come to this school next year?" he asked while looking for another match to set something else on fire.

I made some banal comment.

"If you come here, you might be one of those freshmen who never make it to sophomore year," he said.

"That's right," his partner said.

"You see, some of the brothers like to have cookouts, and what they like to cook and eat are freshmen," the blond boy said. "And they like freshmen about your size."

"They do," said his partner, who was now laughing.

"And the one who eats the most freshmen is Brother Mooney. We call him Monster Mooney."

That was the first time I heard about Monster Mooney, the Christian brother from hell.

At lunch I was laughing with a few of my eighth grade friends about what the kid in the lab had said about Monster Mooney and cannibal cookouts. "I've heard about this Brother Mooney guy," said one of my friends. "I hear he's real mean."

We were seated by a window that overlooked the snowy parking lot, and as we talked, a car drove in and an enormous man, over 300 pounds, got out of the car. As he was walking toward the school, he slipped and fell to the ground. Everyone in the cafeteria started laughing, especially us. The laughter was infectious. But this brother soon got back up on his feet and glared into the window. His eyes were filled with pure evil, and we could see him storm into the building.

"That must be Brother Mooney," said one of my eighth grade friends.

Within seconds, an atmosphere of tension filled the cafeteria. I heard a few mutterings. "Did he see us laugh?"

"He sees everything."

"He knows everything."

And then Brother Mooney was standing in the doorway glaring at all of us. Suddenly, there wasn't a sound in a place where only a minute before there had been uproarious noise. "Bruddah doesn't like to see people laughing at him," he bellowed. A vein was popping out of his neck, and I could see that he had a rather severe overbite. "If Bruddah hears any more noise coming out of this cafeteria, he'll have all of you eat the rest of your lunch in the parking lot, where it's 20 degrees."

And then Brother Mooney turned around and vanished down the hall. I expected to see everyone start laughing and begin making noise again, but for the next ten minutes, until the bell rang, no one spoke.

As we were leaving to go to our next scheduled class, I said to a friend, "That was pretty creepy."

When I started high school the next fall, I didn't see much of Brother Mooney, and halfway through the year he just sort of disappeared.

"Brother Mooney is on retreat," was the official word during a morning announcement, but rumors were rampant.

"I heard they sent him to some fat farm to lose all the weight," one student said.

"I heard he's an alcoholic, and they sent him somewhere to stop drinking," said another.

"I heard he's in jail."

"I heard he doesn't want to be a brother anymore, so he just ran away."

After a while no one talked about him. I didn't really know him, and it didn't seem that any kids really missed him. He just became a missing person. We used to joke that maybe one day his picture would appear on a milk container.

But when I received my class schedule the summer going into tenth grade, I felt a bit queasy because I saw the name of my geometry teacher—Brother Mooney. He was coming back, and I was going to get him.

Life with Brother Mooney. I was a fairly good math student, so my plan was to do my work and not make any trouble. I was the type of kid who usually got along well with his teachers, but because Monster Mooney wasn't a normal teacher, my plan was to be as invisible as possible. I would blend into the desk and not make any eye contact, and the only muscles I would move would be in my right hand when I took notes.

None of us were prepared for what we saw that first day when Brother Mooney stormed into the classroom. He had lost at least 100 pounds, maybe more. Does he have cancer? I wondered. If he did, he looked like he was in the last stages.

We were seated in clusters throughout the classroom when he walked in. "Up front!" he barked, sounding half-human. "Bruddah doesn't like it when you sit so far from him."

A few students in the back moved to some empty seats toward the front of the room. Then he began to take attendance by reading aloud from the alphabetized roll. He mostly read our last names, stopping occasionally to remark, "Are you a jerk like your brother was?" And if anyone said just "Yes" or "No," he would get all over his case about how he was supposed to address him in the proper fashion. "I want you to say, 'Yes, Brother.'" And then we all had to repeat it back to him. "Yes, Brother," we would say.

Fifteen minutes into the first class, it already felt more like boot camp than a tenth grade geometry class, and as the days and weeks began to creep by, the atmosphere never improved. Every morning before class I would start to get a sick sort of feeling in my stomach, and then throughout class I would sit there, hypervigilant about not being noticed. How was I possibly going to make it through an entire year as the invisible boy of geometry class?

And then around October, Brother Mooney's little tortures began. It seemed that he set out each class period to pick on someone, to make a point out of someone else's mistake, or to just plain humiliate someone and prove once again who was the boss.

Usually he picked on some poor slob who didn't have his homework, or a kid who was talking during class and not paying attention. "Jeffrey, I don't see your homework in the pile here," he said one day.

Jeffrey shrugged, "Yeah, I left it at home."

Brother Mooney glared at him.

Jeffrey, now getting a bit flustered, said, "I mean I left it at home, Brother."

"Jeffrey, this will be your new seat," Brother Mooney said, and then he moved a desk right next to his desk.

For the next week, Jeffrey had to sit right next to Monster Mooney, and he received constant reminders to take out his notebook and copy down his notes and make sure he remembered his homework. If I had been Jeffrey, I would have cracked on day two, but somehow that kid got through it.

And there were bigger tortures, even more humiliating. One boy was talking at the beginning of class, and Monster Mooney called him to the front of the room. He drew three circles on the chalkboard, each approximately three feet apart. Then he instructed the boy to put his left index finger in the left circle, his nose in the middle circle and his right index finger in the right circle. He made the boy stand at the board in that fashion with his back to us for the next 40 minutes as the class went back to business. Brother Mooney even wrote notes on the board sometimes right next to the boy and the circles, and every so often he would say to the boy, "How're you feeling?"

"Okay, Brother," the kid would groan, and we would all laugh, mostly out of nervousness.

Another one of his favorite tortures was "Sink the Battleship." If he caught someone misbehaving, he would call the student to the front of the room and draw a battleship on the board. What the student was supposed to do was "sink" the battleship, using his head to completely erase the drawing from the board. He could not return to his seat until the entire outline of that battleship was gone. As the student was doing this, Brother Mooney would be writing notes on the board and teaching the class.

"Brother, I sunk the battleship," the student would say after a few minutes.

Brother Mooney would walk over to the board and then say, "No, I still see the battleship. Keep sinking it!"

Rebellion begins. As Diane Loomans and Karen K. Kolberg write in their book, *The Laughing Classroom,* "a laughing classroom evokes *delightful* forms of play in the learner while a tight-reined classroom evokes *devious* forms of play (a blend of creativity mixed with rebellion)." They also note that the rebel and the class clown have something in common: "They refuse to give in to the joyless grind of learning without spontaneity and laughter."

By the middle of the year, morale in Brother Mooney's class was exceptionally low, and we began to talk about rebellion.

"Maybe we can put a sleeping pill into whatever that crap is that he's drinking," said one student on his way to math class.

"Maybe we can slip fart powder in there," laughed another student.

"Let's let all the air out of his tires."

"Let's put some porn magazines in his desk and then send a tip to the principal."

We didn't end up doing anything, but we would sit in the cafeteria and fantasize about wonderful ways to destroy him and his reputation. We were basically good kids who never got into any trouble, and yet there we would sit, day after day, thinking up ways to destroy this man, a person who was a member of a religious order.

Years later, I can look back and realize that we were merely reflecting back to him the way he was treating us. He constantly put us down, humiliated us, and made us feel powerless, and like any tyrant, all he did was create animosity. We feared him. We did not respect him, and we didn't learn very much geometry that year. All I learned were valuable ways to blend into my environment and not be noticed. I did what was asked of me, did not stand out in any way, and entertained fantasies of great ways to get back at him.

In most school years when I was a boy, I would feel sort of sad when the school year ended. But that year after the final, I just wanted to get away from Brother Mooney. Even during the final exam, I remember he walked around and pointed at mistakes we were making. "Way to go, Varno," he would say to one student. "We spend nine months going over that formula and you still get it wrong."

When he came in my direction, all I could do was try and cover up my test and pray that he wouldn't say anything. I couldn't even think about geometry if he was within ten feet.

Why was he so mean? Why did Brother Mooney treat us this way? When I was a fifteen-year-old schoolboy sitting there day after day, I just figured he was evil, but now I'm a bit wiser in my mid-

40s, and I can see a man who was extremely unhappy. He obviously did not like teaching, at least teaching in an all-boys school. He was burned out and miserable, going through the motions, and not feeling much passion for his career or his life.

It's not surprising that a year later, he disappeared once again, only this time he left with a secretary in the guidance office.

"Did you hear about Monster Mooney? He ran off with Miss Connors, the guidance secretary!" someone said.

The rumors were rampant. I couldn't believe that he would be involved with Miss Connors. In my dealings with her, she was generally happy and smiled fairly frequently. I guess Brother Mooney wasn't having her play "Sink the battleship."

The other teachers and brothers were pretty closed-mouthed about the disappearance of the two of them. Periodically, we would hear rumors—that they were getting married, that they had moved to New Jersey, that Brother Mooney was no longer a brother and was now teaching at another high school. I hope, whatever happened to him, that he found happiness and maybe even became a dad. If he did, I hope the only way he played "sink the battleship" was with his kids when he played the board game, and that he never humiliated another student again. I hope that he journeyed out of the dark side and came into the light.

Creativity not allowed. Before I went to high school, I attended a Catholic elementary school. The nuns who taught me from kindergarten through grade eight were not blessed with tremendous senses of humor or wit. For the most part they were wonderful teachers, but they usually stayed on task. Rarely did we do a lot of laughing.

They liked order, and as a young boy I didn't have too much of a problem with that. I suspect most young kids like to know where the boundaries are at home and at school. With the nuns, you *always* knew where the boundaries were.

I did have a few skirmishes with them. I was the youngest in my family, and I liked to entertain. The nuns weren't particularly fond of entertainers, and I spent quite a few afternoons at "the naughty table" as an early elementary student.

I also tended to see different ways of doing things, and the nuns usually liked us to do things one way—their way. I loved reading and talking about stories and characters and their motives, but the nuns liked more factual questions like, "What was the name of the protagonist's sister?"

Most of my friends wanted to be professional athletes or doctors or firemen or police officers, but I often bragged how I wanted to be a writer. I even entertained my friends with such classic stories as "The Bug Who Ate Albany." They were usually adventure stories with a lot of heads being bitten off and many landmark buildings being destroyed.

One day when I was in fourth grade, we were allowed to get in groups of four and perform a skit about a saint. This was very creative stuff for a Catholic elementary school in the mid-1960s, and I had a ball. My favorite saint was John the Baptist. I liked him because we both had the same first name, and he was a very macho guy who died with a lot of dignity. My play began with his capture and imprisonment, and the conclusion was his decapitation. I was content doing the writing and directing and allowing my other friends to take the starring roles—only a budding writer would do such a thing.

There were about three or four skits that went before us and mostly they, too, were grisly stories about heroic saints who died horrible deaths. However, the teacher didn't let our skit proceed too far after she heard our title. I didn't want to call it "The John the Baptist Story." I wanted a title that would stand out and be dramatic, so I called our skit "I Wish I Had Two Heads." The title elicited a few laughs from my classmates, but the nun wasn't laughing. She didn't like some of the early dialogue either, so after a few minutes, she told our group to sit down. This was the first of many writing rejections, but I tried to take it with dignity.

That evening, the nun even called my house to tell my parents about the title of my story. "John doesn't seem to take his writing very seriously," the nun said, and then went on to tell my dad how the week before when we had to write about what we wanted to be when we grew up, I had written that I wanted to be an adult. When my dad got off the phone, he asked me if I had taken the assignment seriously. "I loved the assignment," I told him. "I loved writing a play, and I didn't want to write some stupid title like everyone else. I think John the Baptist would like the play."
My dad asked to read the play, and I gave it to him.

"Why did you write how you wanted to be an adult when you grew up?" he asked.

"Everyone else was writing about being a teacher or a nurse or a doctor," I said, "so I wanted to write something different, and I figured how bad my life would be if I grew up and didn't become an adult and all my friends did, so that's why I wrote that I wanted to be an adult."

My dad asked to read that story, too, and about an hour later, he stopped by the couch where I was watching television. "These are good stories," he said. "You're a good writer, but maybe for your teacher this year you shouldn't try to be so creative."

Over 30 years later, I think back to that line many times. I don't want any of my students to be in fear of being "so creative."

Classrooms of **LIGHT**

Looking back at the bad examples of teachers in my past helped me decide how I *didn't* want to teach. What could I learn about teaching from the good teachers I'd had in school?

When I thought about teachers I had enjoyed, it occurred to me that I usually received higher grades when the teachers were good ones. Was it the subject or the way they communicated the subject?

I decided that my favorite teachers had made a *connection* with me, usually through humor.

Brother Smith makes an impression. My tenth grade English teacher, Brother Smith, seemed always to know exactly what he was teaching and how he was going to do it. It seemed that he was always fine-tuning each class, throwing out what didn't work and attempting something new and different. He was never bored, and neither were his students.

"It is bad to suppress laughter. It goes back down and spreads to your hips."

– Fred Allen

It was the early 1970s when Brother Smith taught me, and we read and discussed some very edgy stories and books, such as *2001: A Space Odyssey* and *The Exorcist*. He wasn't afraid of controversy, and he would often play popular music of the time by Bob Dylan, Simon and Garfunkel, and Neil Young. We would have intense classroom discussions about what those songs meant, and he loved it when we disagreed with him and could back up our opinions. Brother Smith would also let us select books on our own to read. He borrowed books from us and read and discussed them with us. This made us feel important.

He also had a great sense of humor and enjoyed poking fun at us whenever the opportunity arose, and with tenth graders, that opportunity arose on a daily basis.

We wrote all the time in his class, and he loved reading aloud our work. Sometimes he would read an eloquent piece and praise how good it was, and sometimes he would read an absolutely abysmal piece, and we would laugh and laugh at how bad it was. We never knew who had written either of the pieces, but usually we would admit to the bad writing. We did this because Brother Smith created a safe classroom environment, and his humor never felt mean-spirited, like Brother Mooney's. By getting us to laugh at the poorly written dialogue, the improbable plot and the unbelievable characterizations, he was teaching us how to be critical readers.

We would also get back at Brother Smith whenever possible. Every few weeks, we were given vocabulary words, and it was expected that we would find definitions for them. In class, Brother Smith would call on us to go over the definitions and then use each word correctly in a sentence. We would always try to correctly use the word and at the same time insult Brother Smith.

"All right, the next word is 'lugubrious,'" Brother Smith would say. "Mr. Litynski, please give me the definition."

"It means 'extremely mournful, sad, or gloomy,'" my classmate would respond.

"Okay, now, who can use it correctly in a sentence?" Brother would ask.

Another friend of mine would raise his hand. "Brother Smith's English class always makes me feel lugubrious." And we would all laugh.

We would do this for each word, and sometimes it would be hard to insult Brother Smith with such happy words as "ecstatic" and "blissful," but we would find a way. Part of the fun was to make

Brother Smith laugh. He had a great laugh, and we could all sense that he enjoyed teaching us.

We had so much fun in his class that we never wanted to ruin it by causing any trouble, and he seemed to really care about us. He always wanted to know what books we were reading and what music we were listening to, and he always had seen and was ready to discuss the latest movie playing in local theaters.

I've always felt it is important for a teacher to get to know his or her students, and one way to do this is to be aware of the music they listen to and what movies they enjoy watching. Students want to be validated. They want to be respected for who they are. I might not like rap music or songs by Avril Lavigne, but I should at least be aware of the influence such music has on the students I teach. My job isn't to pretend to be hip and use expressions that seventh and eighth graders use, but I should at least be aware of the culture they are living in.

Brother Mooney would make fun of the music we listened to and the way we dressed and how long we grew our hair. He had an attitude that we were foolish and the things we did weren't worthy of being emulated. Brother Smith, on the other hand, always used our culture as a teaching tool. And when he poked fun at us, it was a gentle, good-natured fun that made us, at times, laugh at ourselves. In turn, he was capable of laughing at his mistakes. If we had ever seen him slip on the ice in the parking lot, he probably would have gotten up and bowed in our direction with a big smile on his face.

Brother Smith was one of the prime reasons I became an English teacher. I had so much fun taking his classes, reading challenging books and stories, having great debates about life and literature, and writing so many different types of stories, poems and essays, that I wanted to keep doing it. English class, taught by Brother Smith, never seemed like work for me, and when I thought about having a career, I thought about doing what he did for the rest of my life. I wanted to stand in front of the classroom and challenge my students, get them excited about literature, encourage them to be creative, and have fun and laugh at the same time.

Getting the good stuff out. Besides wanting to be an English teacher like Brother Smith, I also wanted to be a track and cross-country coach like Brother Mostyn. Brother Mostyn was the vice-principal at my high school, and I had an encounter with him the first day I entered the school as a 4'11" freshman.

My high school was an all-boys school, and there were about 500 students enrolled there, about 498 of them bigger than me. Most of the students had hair down to their shoulders and side-burns growing into their mouths. I had wisps of peach fuzz below my nose. I remember feeling very nervous on that first day.

I had been in school for only one hour before I realized that my locker key was missing. I was sitting in my first period class, and when I put my hand in my pocket to touch the key, there was nothing there. Maybe it had fallen out of my pocket, I thought. Maybe I had dropped it in the hallway? As the teacher droned on about the course requirements, I kept trying to mentally retrace my steps, and gradually I realized what had really happened. I had put my key into the lock, opened the locker, put a few books away, shut the door with my key still in the lock, and then walked to homeroom.

After the class, I raced up the stairs to my locker, hoping, praying, and bargaining with God that my key would still be there.

It was gone.

So now what was I supposed to do? Here it was an hour into my first day of high school, and I had already lost my locker key. I felt like running home. Maybe I was too immature to be in high school. I sure didn't look old enough to be there. Time was ticking away. Students were all heading to their second period classes. Classroom doors were closing all around me.

Maybe someone found the key and brought it to the main office, I hoped.

I opened the heavy wooden door of the main office and walked inside, still not quite sure what I would say. There were four or five big, hairy students standing in there talking to one of the secretaries. They all turned their heads and looked down at me. "What can I do for you? Are you lost?" asked a secretary with a gravelly voice.

I swallowed hard. The words, "I lost my locker key," came out of my mouth, but I wasn't so sure I had spoken them.

Everyone, even the secretary, laughed. She moved her head to her right and said, "Brother Mostyn, did you hear this? We have a young man out here who has lost his locker key."

A tall, somewhat balding brother, wearing black pants and a black shirt, walked out of his office. He was holding black glasses in his right hand, and he scratched his graying goatee with his left hand. He put the glasses on and looked at me. "Come into my office," he said and then sort of smiled.

I followed him in.

"What's your name?" he asked and sat on the edge of his desk. His room was covered with master schedules taped up on every wall.

"Jack Rightmyer," I said.

He motioned for me to sit, and I did. "What happened, Jack?"

I tried to swallow. Then I told him.

Brother Mostyn reached out his hand. "Well, Jack, congratulations. You've set the all-time record for losing a locker key." I shook his hand and even smiled, sort of.

We went back out into the main office. He found another locker key for me, told me that I would have to pay $5.00 for the missing key, and said I would have to switch to another locker just in case someone had kept my old key. I just nodded my head in agreement.

We went out into the hallway and walked upstairs to my locker. Walking with him was like walking with a rock star or a famous politician. He seemed to know every student by name, and every student seemed to know him. As we walked, he asked me a few questions about my family, where I lived, and what my favorite subjects were. We got to my locker. He opened it with a master key, and then we went to another empty locker not too much further down the hall, and he helped me move my belongings into the new locker.

"Do you like any sports?" he asked.

"I like baseball, basketball, golf—just about every sport," I told him.

"Did you ever think about going out for cross-country or track?" he asked. I shook my head no. "I'm the cross-country and track coach, and I think you would be a good runner."

"I'm not much of a runner," I told him, "but I'm a pretty good basketball player. I'm going to try out for the hoops team in November."

"Well, Jack, I hope you make the team, but if you ever change your mind, let me know."

Every day after that, whenever I passed by Brother Mostyn in the crowded hallway, he would always smile, call me by name and say hello. I was only a puny freshman, but somehow he had made me feel important.

Basketball tryouts. The freshman school days seemed to go by quite fast. Every afternoon that fall when I got home from school, I would head out to my backyard and start shooting baskets. I was working on my jump shot and trying to learn how to shoot with my left hand.

And then November came, along with tryouts for the ninth grade basketball team. I stood in line with 50 other freshmen, listening to Coach Reynolds call out our names. The line stretched almost the entire length of the basketball court. "We've got too many people trying out," screamed Coach Reynolds. "Tomorrow I'll invite back only 18 of you."

My mouth was dry. I gulped.

"I'm looking for two things," continued the coach. "I'm looking for height and speed."

I caught myself moving up on my toes.

We then began doing an assortment of drills—running, passing, dribbling, and sprinting. The freshman and varsity coaches sat at a table by half-court and watched us play. What were they writing down? What were they whispering?

For the last 30 minutes, we were broken up into two different half-court scrimmage games. My heart was pounding away as I passed the ball to a guard who dribbled slowly toward the hoop. I jogged beside him, and the coaches yawned at the table. My strategy was "Don't make a mistake," and I didn't. I made some nice passes, moved the ball well, and even tossed up a 15-foot jump shot that swished right through.

"Tomorrow morning, I'll post the 18 names outside my office," shouted Coach Reynolds as we left the court.

Oh, God, please don't let me get cut, I kept thinking. Please give me a chance. I want to be a part of some team. I don't want to go home on the bus every day after school.

I could barely sleep that night. All I thought about was basketball. My nervous stomach kept doing flips all night and all morning as I tried to swallow some breakfast.

When the bus dropped me off at school, I raced inside. I joined the hoard of hoopers, and we stood crowded together as Coach Reynolds came out of his office and tacked the small piece of paper onto the bulletin board. As usual, the names were in alphabetical order. Mine wasn't there. I wanted to ask, "Are these the people who were cut?" I wanted to yell out, "You'll regret this. You've made a horrible mistake."

Some kids were grumbling. "I knew I'd get cut," laughed one.

"It was all rigged," another said.

My eyes were watery, but I tried to hold my head up as I walked out into the crowded hallway. There was a poster on the bulletin board next to my homeroom. "Join the indoor track team," it read. "Come to a meeting on Friday in Room 25. All are invited."

I sat down in my assigned homeroom seat. "All are invited," I kept thinking. I wouldn't have to go home on the bus every day. I could be part of *something*.

All are invited. I thought back to that summer when I had come home from playing golf with my friends and turned on the TV to watch some of the 1972 Munich Summer Olympics. There was an American named Frank Shorter running all alone through the city streets with "USA" proudly showing on his chest.   I decided to join the indoor track team.

The track team. I immediately became the worst runner on the team. Still, after each race, Brother Mostyn found something encouraging to say. I also made a whole new set of friends, and my life changed forever.

And as a senior, after four years of hard training filled with many disappointments and many ecstatic races and much laughter, I broke the school record for the two-mile run. I walked up to Brother Mostyn, who was beaming with pride at my success, and thanked him.

"Thanks for being such a great coach," I said.

"You did all the work," he said.

"And thanks for believing in me and encouraging me to come out for track and cross-country on my first day when I lost my locker key. Thanks for not yelling at me and making me feel bad." I was trying real hard to not get too corny, but I had just beaten one of our oldest school records, and I was feeling pretty nostalgic. "And thanks for getting to know my name when I was a puny little freshman. You made me feel important."

Brother Mostyn smiled. "Of course I wanted you to run cross-country and track. I could tell when you walked in that office that there was nothing phony about you. You never gave me some long story about losing your locker key. You just told me the truth, and that took some guts. But I never knew you'd be a good runner—that happened because you worked at it. I just knew that a kid with your attitude was the type of kid I like to coach. You made yourself into a good runner because you believed it could happen. You came to practice and worked hard every day. As a teacher for all these years, I've found that there's a lot of good in everybody. My job is to try and get that good stuff out."

Over 25 years later, I keep thinking of that statement: how a teacher's job is to try and get that good stuff out of every student he or she meets. That's not a bad mission statement for all of us involved in education.

Finding my **WAY**

My dad was an accountant, but at the dinner table and whenever I was around him, he never once talked about accounting. However, he loved talking about the latest book he was reading. That was where his passion was, in literature. At the age of 18, I knew enough to major in the area where I felt my passion. I wanted to be an English teacher so I could read and write and get into lively discussions. "And they would pay me to do this?" I thought. "Not bad!"

But when I eventually stood in front of real students in a real classroom, I wondered how I could create this passion, this love of literature and writing, with my teaching style. I wanted to be like Brother Smith and Paul O'Brien, and I wanted to be that good right now.

The truth is that I needed to serve my apprenticeship. I needed to learn on the job. I needed to learn the material.

"Good teaching is one-fourth preparation and three-fourths theater."

– Gail Godwin

Learning to relax. As my first year progressed, I began to relax a bit more. I began to gain some confidence in my abilities. Paul showed me that a teacher doesn't have to know everything. If a student asked me a question and I didn't know the answer, I learned to say, "I'll look that up and get back to you tomorrow."

This was a tough hurdle for me because I was the teacher and I was supposed to know everything about the subject of English. My parents had just spent all this money on my college education, but I was starting to realize that I didn't know a lot. Today I call this *wisdom.* In my early twenties, finding out that I didn't actually know very much was a shock. At the time, I thought I was just plain dumb.

I don't think I was ever really myself during my first year of teaching, until the very end of the year. One day I admitted to Paul, "I don't know what to do with my seniors for the next few days since I've taught everything that's on their final and we've already reviewed for the test. They just want to graduate and go to college. I don't know how I can keep their attention right now."

Paul smiled and said, "Hey, you just graduated from college a year ago, and most of them will be going to college in a few months. Why not ask them if they have any questions about college? You know, like what to expect, what living in a dorm is like."

I decided to give it a shot.

When my seniors came to class, I summoned up my courage and said, "Today I'm not going to be Mr. Rightmyer. I'm going to be a person who just graduated from college and has come here to answer any questions you have about what it's like to be a college student."

Immediately the room quieted down. Students began looking at each other, perhaps wondering if I had suffered some type of nervous breakdown. Someone sheepishly put his hand up in the back of the room and asked me what college I went to and what I liked about it.

"I went to Manhattan College," I said, "and I liked going to school in New York City and living on my own and making a whole bunch of new friends."

More silence. The students were still looking around the room shrugging their shoulders. Another raised hand from the back.

"Was college hard?"

"I found it hard as a freshman," I said, "but then I started figuring out how to take notes and how to write papers and how to pace myself with all my free time. I ended up becoming a pretty good student."

"Did you party every night?" asked one of the class troublemakers, and everyone began laughing.

"No, if I partied every night I wouldn't be here today," I laughed. "I'd probably be in some alcohol rehab place or maybe on the five-year plan at my college. But I partied every weekend and on most Thursday nights." This was met with a large chorus of laughter and a few "Mr. Rightmyer parties!"

And that's how it went for the next 40 minutes—some serious questions addressing honest concerns about college and dorm life, and a few ridiculous questions. I answered them all as honestly as I could. I was relaxed and joked with them, and we laughed and smiled.

It was my favorite class of the year. When the bell rang, I had a group of students that even hung around my desk and kept talking. That hadn't happened all year. Usually when one of my classes came to an end, all the students disappeared quickly out the door and down the hall. But hanging around to chat with me? That was something I saw the students do in Paul's classroom all the time, and it felt good. I imagined myself as Mr. Chips at that English boarding school.

What happened that day was that I truly connected with my students. I didn't hide behind my barrier as "teacher." I looked them in the eye. I relaxed. I joked and laughed and was real. They responded back to me the same way.

Twenty-eight years later. It took me one full year to begin to unravel the mystery of how to start being a good teacher. Today, 28 years later, I still fall into bad habits like thinking, "I must get through this novel, and I haven't taught them how to write dialogue, and how can they possibly move on to eighth grade if they don't know what a split infinitive is?"

That's when I remind myself that I'm teaching individuals and not machines. I'm teaching a roomful of people who learn in different ways and at different times. I need to remember to communicate with them. I need to allow them to feel safe because that's when real learning takes place.

Now I always have a good day, although some afternoons I shuffle off to the parking lot, exhausted. I enjoy my colleagues. I enjoy my students, even the difficult ones. I enjoy the challenge of teaching, getting young people to think and write creatively. I enjoy seeing my students take risks and try something brand new. I don't always enjoy correcting papers and calculating grades—actually I despise grading—but what job is perfect? As they say, "We call it work for a reason."

Most important, today I have fun doing what I do. I know that when I'm relaxed and enjoying myself, my students are likely to enjoy themselves, too.

What Makes a **GOOD TEACHER?**

What makes a good teacher? Numerous studies have shown that teachers need to establish a classroom climate that minimizes discipline problems and encourages academic excellence. Teachers should know their subjects, and they should not lecture every day.

For years, however, I've been doing my own study. Every year I ask my students to describe the perfect classroom atmosphere and to write about a teacher who has made a difference in their life. They always refer to an atmosphere that's relaxed. They always go on and on about teachers who have made a difference to them. Here is what they have had to say over the years about good teachers:

"When humor goes, there goes civilization."

– Erma Bombeck

- They are smart. They know their subject.
- They are nice.
- They make learning fun.
- They don't give pointless homework or busy work just to keep you quiet.
- They don't give any homework.
- They have blond hair.
- They're pretty.
- They smell good.
- They're funny.
- You can laugh in their class.
- They don't yell.
- They discipline students without embarrassing them.
- They make you want to come to class.
- They challenge you to think differently.

These are responses from seventh grade students and I think they're pretty much on the money— well, except for having blond hair or being pretty. These are ordinary kids from all economic and ethnic backgrounds listing characteristics of teachers who have made a difference in their lives. If you think about a teacher who made a difference in your life, that teacher probably had some of the same characteristics my students write about every year.

I also have my students write about a teacher that did *not* connect well with them. I don't want to call them bad teachers, but let's admit it: there are far too many bad teachers out there. I prefer to call them "teachers we did not connect with," and I always tell my students I don't want their names, what subjects they teach, or what grades they teach. I don't even want to know if they're male or female. Here are some of the responses I receive year after year about these other teachers:

- They are boring.
- They don't know your name till December.
- They have bad breath.
- They yell.
- They like failing you.
- They don't give you a second chance.
- They're mean.
- They're unorganized.
- They tell you their personal problems.
- They give too much homework and too much busy work.

Again, I think the students are right on the money.

Boring? I know many teachers are boring. Heck, I'm boring myself a lot of the time. I tell my students that I'm a teacher, not an entertainer, but I try to create a lively class, and many days they are the ones I'm relying on to keep the energy level up. "So if I'm boring," I tell them, "it's up to you guys to get some action going, think out of the box, take some risks, and help make this class more fun." Any actor, musician or comic will tell you that the best performances come in front of the best audiences.

Most of the other qualities students listed come down to issues of communication and personality. A successful teacher needs to make a connection with students. You don't do this by telling them your personal problems or becoming their friend. You do it by learning their names as quickly as possible, by showing them you care about them, by being patient and giving them a second chance on occasion, by listening to them, by being compassionate, by being organized and knowledgeable about your subject. (Teaching sounds like such an easy job now, doesn't it? It's no wonder we're losing so many young teachers after only three years.)

Finally, the comment, "They like failing you," always surprises me. I've taught in many different schools and known many different teachers, but I have yet to encounter any teacher who actually *liked* failing a student. How sad it is that some students really believe teachers must hang out somewhere in the faculty room and drool over poor test grades and compete with each other about failing the most students.

Finding what suits your personality. Every few years a new philosophy about education storms the country and promises to be the best way to reach children and improve our educational system. I've been through Paideia, Madeline Hunter, and "whole language." Now we're into the era of state testing and high standards. All these trends have positive elements to them, but classroom teachers still need to find their own best personal way to reach students. We need to find what suits our own personality.

It took me a while, but what worked for my personality was a relaxed classroom atmosphere where I could use humor as a way to communicate my subject to the high school and middle school students I've taught through the years. The degree of humor in the class varies year to year, based on the classroom personalities of my students, but for me to enjoy my teaching, I know I need to laugh and have fun and create an atmosphere of spontaneity.

Learning to **LAUGH**

Using humor. For me, part of becoming comfortable in the class-room involved learning to see the power of humor. When my tenth graders read *Huckleberry Finn*, I eventually decided to play a recording of Hal Holbrook doing his one-man Mark Twain show. The kids loved it. Their laughter was contagious, and as we laughed, I physically felt better.

It makes sense. Research in the past 20 years has shown the physical benefits of laughing. Some of the findings:

"Humor is the great thing, the saving thing, after all. The minute it crops up, all our hardnesses yield, all our irritations and resentments slip away, and a sunny spirit takes their place."

– Mark Twain

- Laughter reduces stress.
- It increases immune defenses.
- It improves respiration.
- It improves circulation.
- It increases pain threshold.
- It makes you more alert.
- It improves your memory.

I felt better while the class was laughing. I also noticed my students seemed more focused and seemed to retain the information better. Weeks later, they were still talking about what Hal Holbrook had said in that recording.

After we read *Huckleberry Finn*, we moved on to *The Catcher in the Rye*. I remembered reading the book as a sophomore in high school and being amazed that we got to read a book in school with words like "fart" and all that swearing. And it was laugh-out-loud funny. Paul O'Brien read aloud some of the best parts in his class, even with all the swear words, but I chickened out and only read aloud some of the tamer parts. But still, my classes were laughing and having a great time reading those two books.

Occasionally on a half day, a day teachers sometimes call a wasted day, I would try some humor, some funny poems or funny articles I had found. The classes usually loved them, but I wasn't sure if they were more focused because it was a half day and they were just in a good mood, or if it had something to do with the material itself.

Today I know that humor has a lot of power. It can improve the educational atmosphere of the classroom. It can also be a strong determiner in keeping teachers from burning out.

How do you use humor effectively? Ronald A. Berk, in his book, *Humor as an Instructional Defibrillator*, talks about ways to use humor to connect with students and engage them in learning. Here are some of the important findings he's discovered about humor in the classroom:

- Creating humor involves releasing the childlike imagination that seems to get repressed as we age.
- Humor breaks down barriers that can separate students and teachers. A connection between students and the teacher is critical for learning to take place.
- Positive humor is not based on intimidation.
- Humor can bring your students to life and energize them.
- Laughter occurs in casual, relaxed environments.
- Laughter is contagious.
- Eye contact increases laughter.

- Humor prevents job burnout.
- Positive humor will increase a student's self-esteem.

While humor can be powerful, it also has a downside. According to Berk, inappropriate humor can cause students to become withdrawn and feel resentment, anger, tension, and/or anxiety.

There is no way a teacher will be able to connect with a student who feels this way in class, and there is no way a student who feels this way will perform well and learn in class.

Because inappropriate humor has such negative side effects, it is, of course, important that students know the difference. I have found out the hard way that students don't necessarily know which type of humor is appropriate or inappropriate.

During the first few days of class, when I go over the classroom rules, I make a point of telling my classes, "I like to run a relaxed atmosphere in here, but that's something you can't abuse. I like to laugh, and I like to see you laugh, but I will not put up with any inappropriate humor toward me or toward anyone in this classroom or this school. I then ask the students, "What is inappropriate humor?"

Every year in every class, my students always come up with correct answers. "Dumb blonde jokes," says one student.

"That's right," I say. "Anytime we're laughing at another person's expense, that's inappropriate humor."

"Making fun of someone who's Polish or a different race," says another student.

"Yes, that's put-down humor again," I say.

"Making fun of old drivers and old people," says another student.

"Making fun of what someone's wearing or where they live or what their hair looks like."

"Or if they're losing their hair," I say and get some laughter when I point out my bald spot.

"Insult humor can be bad," says another student.

A student in the back of the room jumps into the conversation. "I like insult humor with my friends, but I don't like it with someone I don't know."

I tell the students that sometimes insult humor between good friends can be acceptable if you feel very safe. "You know the insult humor isn't the truth," I say, "and your friend is using it to get you to laugh. Sometimes guys, especially, do this, but you're right when you say insult humor from a person you don't know is inappropriate because you don't feel safe."

I know I need to create a safe environment by making my students understand the difference between appropriate and inappropriate humor. Then they, and I, can be more playful. As educational guru Maria Montessori has written, "True learning always takes place in a spirit of joy and abandonment."

Humor enhances learning. Dr. Joel Goodman, the founder and director of The Humor Project (www.HumorProject.com), located in Saratoga Springs, New York, believes that using humor to enhance learning isn't just a gimmick. "Humor captures and maintains attention and reduces tension," he says. "As a result, retention goes up."

If you want to inject some laughter into your lessons, Goodman says it is important to consider the suggestions below.

1. Avoid humor that doesn't fit your personality. Ask yourself, "What makes me laugh?" I love zany, ridiculous humor that you can find in Monty Python films and *Naked Gun* movies. This is perfect humor for teaching at the middle school level. It's the type of humor that looks at the absurdity of everyday life, and it's the type of humor I grew up with in my family and with my friends. However, put-down humor used by comedians like Don Rickles is something I don't like, and it wouldn't work for me to use that kind of humor with my students.

2. Don't think that you must do stand-up comedy. When I address my students at the beginning of each class and after a weekend, I often discuss some funny things I've seen or done. However, I never feel like I'm doing a monologue. It's my way of reaching the class and easing them into the nuts and bolts of what today's class will be all about.

Another thing I've done to lighten the atmosphere is to simply surprise students with the unexpected. For example, students everywhere enter the classroom and say, "What are we going to do today?"

When I first started teaching, I would announce everything that I had planned for that day. "We're going to do a journal entry and then read and discuss a poem about a basketball player."

A student would scrunch up her nose and say something like, "I hate poetry, and I hate basketball."

For a few years, to avoid such unpleasantness, I would pretend not to even hear the question. I would stick my head into a plan book or pretend to take attendance. If the student continued to badger me, I would say something like, "If you take your seat and open your notebook, I'll begin class and then you'll find out what we're going to do."

This response often sounded a bit arrogant and usually left the student feeling sort of put off. And that's when I came up with another approach.

"What are we gonna do in class today, Mr. Rightmyer?"

"I don't know," I would say. "I'm making it up as I go along."

That got a few chuckles and seemed to work for a while, but then students began asking me, "What are we doing today, or are you still just making it up as you go along?"

And my responses began to get even more outrageous. "Today we're going to learn how to make balloon animals."

"Today we're going to build a kayak."

"Today we're going to try out my time machine that I bought over the weekend."

For some students, this is one of the highlights of the class. What crazy response will Mr. Rightmyer come up with next?

3. Begin with gradual and low-risk humor intervention, such as a lapel button or funny signs around the classroom. It's not my style to wear funny buttons, but I certainly have some funny posters and comic strips displayed around the room, and I always have a funny day-to-day desk calendar that most students rush to and read at the beginning of class. It's my way of alerting them that we are in a classroom that allows laughter.

4. Prime the humor pump with bulletin board items, and encourage students to bring in humor. I enjoy putting funny items on my bulletin board throughout the year, and I'll display funny cartoons and drawings my students have made themselves, showing them I value and appreciate their work and their sense of humor. I don't try to be their buddy or their friend, but I do feel it's important for me to make a connection with them.

5. Have humor rituals, such as a funny quote of the day. I've never had humor rituals, but on occasion I will begin a class by reading a top ten list from a David Letterman show or a funny quote from George Carlin, Jerry Seinfeld, John Stewart, or Steven Colbert. The quote usually has something to do with what we'll be doing that day in class.

6. Stick with positive forms of humor. Sarcasm only fuels revenge. It's very important that humor in the classroom is positive. Adolescence is one of the most insecure times of our lives, and I don't want to make my students feel any worse by poking fun at them in a sarcastic way.

I also feel that putting someone else down is a sure way of showing your own insecurity. A teacher has a responsibility to demonstrate humor that's appropriate. I'm being paid as a teacher, not as a stand-up comedian, and my students are teenagers who are there to learn. They are not drunken patrons at a Las Vegas show.

7. Don't use more humor in the first part of the year than you expect to use later on. I think I use my humor pretty evenly throughout the school year, but I also know there are some classes and some years where I can't use as much humor as I would like because my students aren't capable of laughing and then transitioning back to our lesson. When my students are already revved up, such as the days before a school vacation, I won't use as much humor because I might not be able to rein them in. But the day or two after we've returned from a long break and students are down in the dumps—that's a perfect time to spice up the class with some humor.

8. Take author Susan RoAne's AT & T test. Is it Appropriate, Timely, and Tasteful? The more that humor can be related to the subject matter, the better. Though my humor is always tasteful and appropriate, sometimes my jokes or pithy statements might go over the heads of my students. That's okay, though. We all have both hits and misses.

9. Most important: Be willing to laugh at yourself. I once taught half of a class period with my pants zipper down. A student sitting up front discreetly tried to let me know, but I wasn't picking up on any of his obvious gestures. It took the class clown to finally raise his hand and say, "Your zipper is down."

Being the experienced teacher that I was, I quickly said, "Very funny. Do you really think I'm going to fall for that corny joke?"

And that's when the entire class began to laugh, and I suddenly felt a noticeable breeze shoot through my pants. With a quick look, I noticed that my zipper was not only down, but my dress shirt was also sticking out of the opening. All I could do was laugh, pull up my zipper, and try in my most professional way to move on to the next portion of the class. What else could I do? We're all human beings, and we all have ridiculous things happen to us. We might as well laugh at them.

Humor as stress relief. Dr. Goodman feels that humor is a great way to relieve stress both in the classroom and in the teachers' lounge. "Research has shown that humor belongs in the teachers' faculty room as well as in the classroom," he said. "A longitudinal Harvard study determined that a sense of humor is a key reason why stress doesn't kill more quickly and commonly."

According to Dr. Goodman, humor in the teachers' lounge will curtail some of the teachers' lounge syndrome of moaning and groaning, which can ruin anyone's day. As Paul O'Brien said to me numerous times, "There are some teachers hanging out in the faculty room who are so full of life that you just find yourself being pulled toward them, and there are others who are so depressing that you find yourself running away from them."

One I always enjoyed was an English teacher named Dominick who had an irreverent sense of humor. He was a great wit who had the ability to see through all the phoniness of life and school. One of the traditions he started was to take 45 or 50 of the already-used high school yearbook pictures of the staff and students and display them on poster boards with hilarious comments underneath. He would leave these in the faculty room on one of the last school days of the year, and we would laugh all day at how perfect his captions were.

Humor connects. Margie Ingram, the vice president and coordinator of The Humor Project's annual international conference, says

"Humor connects people, reduces our stress, and can physically make us feel better." She believes we can learn to take our jobs seriously and ourselves lightly. "Television sitcoms and comedy films are funny," she says, "but if we learn to observe humor all around us, then we'll laugh through much of the day. The more we look for humor, the more we'll see it."

Our students go through a typical school day bombarded by facts in English, math, social studies, science, and sometimes physical education, art, music, technology, foreign languages, and other subjects. If we want students to see the importance of learning, we need to present information in as lively and as passionate a way possible. Humor often helps students connect information to their lives.

Students also don't just need information, they need information that is really going to matter to them. When I was in elementary school, I found the language arts portion of the day very dull because all we usually did was diagram sentences. We also did grammar exercises out of a book, one example after another. I would sit in the class and count through the book and find the number I was going to be called on to answer. I would just sit there and wait for my turn to answer that question and then go back into my trance-like state until the next number I was called on to answer. Very dull. Very boring. We did little real writing, and when we read a story, we always discussed the facts of the story. Who was the main character? Where did the family live? We never talked about stuff I was interested in, such as why the characters acted a certain way and what the author was trying to get the reader to think about. I found that stuff important and interesting, and I also enjoyed *writing* sentences, not diagramming them.

Why should young people trust knowledge that brings no joy and excitement to their lives? All the research has shown that real learning takes place when people have a real motivation to learn it. Real learning happens when students have a love for something and want to find out everything they can about it. Our job as teachers is to try to create an atmosphere that will motivate our students and do what Brother Mostyn always tried to do: "Get that good stuff out."

Choose Your ATTITUDE

The film *Fish! Catch the Energy. Release the Potential.* was the inspiration for the famous FISH! philosophy described in a number of best-selling books, including *FISH! Sticks* and *FISH! for Life*. The FISH! philosophy is a prescription for a work life that balances teamwork, joy, productivity and passion. It was inspired by the fishmongers at Seattle's Pike Place Fish Market. Despite working in cold, wet, smelly conditions, the employees bring a sense of joy to their work each day, throwing fish at one another, making spectacular catches, and delighting their customers. According to one of the Fish! principles, *you* choose your attitude for the day, and if you don't like your attitude, *you* can choose another one. Not long ago, I decided to put this principle to work.

"Life should be lived as play."

–Plato

One of the big stressors in my life is my daily commute to work. I must admit that being caught in a traffic jam in the morning can usually send my blood pressure soaring. I'm not one of these people who needs to get to work an hour before I have to, but some days I'm walking into school with the kids.

My wife often told me to relax in the mornings. "But it's snowy today," I would say, "and the traffic is going to be brutal, and I have to get to school before all the buses because they take forever dropping off the students, and if I don't get there on time I might not even get a parking space. Maybe I should just buy a cot and an electric stove and live in my classroom during the winter. I live too far from school. Thirty miles is such a waste of time and gas."

"Do you think Martin Luther King or Mahatma Gandhi complained all the time?" asked my wife. "Just be happy you have a job you like and that you do it well."

Attitude improvement. As usual, my wife was right. I needed to choose a better attitude, so one day I stopped by the local library and checked out an audio self-help tape called *Learning How to Live Your Best Life*.

The authors of this tape had once written a best-selling book about the power of a positive attitude. Their new book/tape guaranteed that it would teach me the meaning of life. It would also show me how to forgive myself and others and how to turn my mistakes into opportunities for growth. All of this would be accomplished in two 60-minute audio tapes.

The next morning at the breakfast table, I informed my family that I was going to become an enlightened being.

"Where are the comics?" asked my son. That's the only part of the newspaper he ever read.

"It's my day to sit next to the heater," my daughter said. For added emphasis, she began shivering.

"You really need to get some salt for that walkway," my wife said. "The paperboy almost fell and got hurt this morning."

I guess they weren't too interested in hearing about *Learning How to Live Your Best Life*, but in a few days, when they saw the changes in me, they would be curious.

The new me sets off to work. As the darkness began to fade outside, I could see that once again it was snowing. There wasn't enough snow to get a day off or even a delay, but there was enough to make the morning commute miserable. I ate as quickly as I could and then announced to my family, "I'd better leave early because the Northway is going to be a parking lot."

My family quietly moved out of my way, and then for the next 15 minutes, I searched the house for my car keys. Feeling a scream slowly building in my throat, out of desperation, I asked my wife if she had seen them.

"Why don't you check the pockets of your coat?" she said and went back to drinking her coffee.

"I never leave them in the pockets of my coat," I grumbled.

To humor her, I decided to check there anyway, and sure enough, that's where they were. Breathing deeply, I moved quickly around the table and gave everyone a quick kiss. I raced outside, almost fell on the steps, realized I should definitely get salt, and proceeded to warm up the car and scrape the ice from the windshield. Since it was getting late, I decided to scrape enough just to peek out. I then jumped into the car and drove away.

Unfortunately, before I had traveled 100 yards, the windshield steamed up and I had to stop the car, get out and finish scraping. It was now 6:45. But even with the snow, I figured I could still get to school with a few minutes to spare.

The icebox of a car was now giving off some faint whispers of heat, but my toes were still frozen. I popped in the first tape and settled back for a relaxing drive to work. "You are an important part of the universe," the voice said. "The world would not be as good a place if you weren't in it."

I smiled when I heard this, since I had always suspected this was true. But my smile turned to a sneer when I got stuck behind a local school bus. It was parked on the road waiting for some kid to come out of his house. This child is a menace, I thought. He's going to cause all of us to to be late.

"Negative thoughts destroy the inner peace that is found within all of us," the voice said over the beautiful background noise of a soft guitar and sounds of water running down rocks.

It was now 7:00 a.m., and I forced myself to think positive thoughts. I didn't even yell at the kid when he stumbled down his driveway to the bus. I even waved to him. Seconds later, his mother came running down the driveway after him to give him his lunch, and I even tried to force a smile in her direction. She walked up the steps of the bus and seemed to take forever getting the lunch to the boy, and I attempted to hold my smile as I watched this show. But my eyes kept glancing at the ticking minute hand of my car's clock.

The Northway was slow going, but at least cars were moving. "Successful people are the ones who perform well during times of adversity," said the voice. A massive truck drove by, spraying dirty slush onto my windshield. I used the wiper to get it off but soon realized I was out of washer fluid. This was a time of adversity, so I decided not to panic and drove close behind other trucks, using their spray to keep my windshield semi-clean.

The parking lot began at Exit 8A, which was a newly built ramp that was supposed to relieve traffic congestion but only created more congestion. I looked at the other drivers around me. Most of them were twitching or running their hands through their hair. It's too bad they weren't listening to *Learning How to Live Your Best Life*, I thought. I wanted to tell them not to think negative thoughts.

It was now 7:30.

By the time I got off the Northway, I had ten minutes to get to school. Even with the snow coming down and cars off the road and in ditches, I began driving faster. I was now moving my hands through my hair, just like all the other drivers. I decided to yank *Learning How to Live Your Best Life* out of the car stereo and put in something a bit more energetic, something by the Ramones.

I drove my car, with its filthy windshield, into the school parking lot like it was the last lap of the Indy 500. It was now 8:05. I ran into the school, crashing my way through the horde of students. "You're late, Mr. Rightmyer," one of them said. "Did you over-sleep?" another asked.

Part of me wanted to scream, but I smiled instead and tried to prevent negative and murderous thoughts from entering my head.

My homeroom students were all waiting out in the hallway. A cheer went up when they saw me walk toward them. "You're here," one student said.

"We didn't know what to do," another said.

"That's because I'm an important part of the universe," I answered, "and the world would not be as good a place if I wasn't in it."

The students exchanged worried glances, and that's when I noticed Rich, one of my fellow teachers, walking by my room. He still had his coat on, and I saw that his homeroom students were also out-side his room at the far end of the hallway. But Rich didn't seem so worried. He didn't have the deer in the headlights look which I know I had on my face. He smiled at me and laughed with a few of the stu-dents who were walking with him down the hall, as I hyperventilated and tried to open the door to my homeroom.

Rich strolled down the hall, apparently without one concern about being late. Later, I asked him about it. "On that snowy morn-ing when you came in late, why did you seem so relaxed?"

He smiled. "I realized a long time ago that life is all about your attitude. Do you wake up in the morning happy to get out of bed, or do you want to stay in bed and not leave your house? It's attitude. It's the same way with being late or being early. There are a lot of people who rush into this building acting like they're late, even though they're 15 minutes early. My feeling is, you're only late if you act late, and on days when I'm late, I stroll in like I'm on time."

You're only late if you act late, I thought, and I began laughing. I decided to bring *Learning How to Live Your Best Life* back to the library even though I had not heard the last 60-minute tape. I much preferred what this teacher said about attitude. From that day on, whenever I'm late, I stroll into school with my head held high, saying "hello" to my fellow teachers and any students I come upon. When my students say, "You're late, Mr. Rightmyer." I tell them, "You're only late when you act late."

Being **PLAYFUL**

I grew up in a family that was filled with laughter. Our favorite TV shows were comedies, and at dinner we would usually have some laughs about funny things that happened during the day. I always felt drawn to the type of kid who looked at things in a different way. These kids were usually very funny. (Sometimes they didn't even know how funny they were.) Their humor was natural, not forced. It was playful.

> *"It is easy to work when the soul is at play."*
>
> – Emily Dickinson

My friends and I also tended to enjoy teachers who dressed differently, acted a bit differently and seemed to enjoy themselves. I guess you could say my family, my friends, and my favorite teachers and coaches all knew how to be playful.

The definition of the word *play* is "to take part in an enjoyable activity for the sake of amusement." That basically sums up what my favorite people do on a daily basis. As my father once said, "We're all gonna die someday, so we might as well have as much fun as we can when we're alive."

I should have remembered his advice when I began teaching, but I fell into believing that fun could not happen at work. What a mistake that was. It should have occurred to me that I had been having fun most of my life at home, at school, on vacations and in sports, so why couldn't I also have fun at work?

A playful family. As a boy, I had a front row seat to the many characters who were my relatives. Uncle Charlie lived next door and used to sit out underneath his willow tree smoking cigarettes and swearing at the mosquitoes. His wife, my Aunt Stella, used to swear so much that her parakeet, Pete, swore right along with her. And right in my own house was my father, a long-suffering Boston Red Sox fan who would sit outside night after night and listen to his boys play on radio station WTIC from Hartford, Connecticut, over two hours away. While other fathers in my neighborhood were working on their car engines or mowing the lawn, my dad would sit outside in the same spot, night after night, listening to games on a cheap radio with aluminum foil on the antenna. "It gets the best reception," he would tell me. He would listen through the static and sometimes not even know the score of the game because signals from other stations would occasionally creep in.

"What's the score of the game, Dad?" I would ask.

"I don't know," he would say. "I think the Red Sox have six, and it's going to rain tomorrow in Toronto."

All of these people had a sense of fun about them, which is an important ingredient for all teachers, coaches, doctors, nurses and probably people in every occupation. Maybe funeral directors shouldn't be playful, but I'm sure even a few of them would disagree with me.

Finding the fun kids. In high school I found that a high percentage of fun kids were the distance runners who ran on the cross-country and track teams. That was one of the reasons I joined the indoor track team as a freshman. (Okay, the main reason was that I had just been cut from the basketball team, and there were no cuts on the indoor track team. If I wanted to play a sport that winter it had to be track.)

I didn't mind running track since I had visions of one day becoming an Olympic marathon runner. I wanted to have as much fun as Frank Shorter looked like he was having when he ran all alone through the streets of Munich in 1972, almost smiling when he entered the Olympic Stadium as a winner. Now if that had been me, I would have been pumping my arms and blowing kisses at the crowd. I used to practice doing that on some nightly runs through my neighborhood.

Anyway, that's what I wanted to do—be an Olympic marathon winner. But first I had to learn how to run one mile. After the first 15 minutes of our opening practice, I realized that running distance looked a lot easier on television than it did in real life. I was not only the worst runner on the team, I was arguably the worst runner in the northern hemisphere. In my first indoor track race as a freshman, I finished 24th out of 25 in the mile with a time of 6:34. The guy I beat had dropped out.

On the drive home my dad was quite impressed that I had run an entire mile and not stopped. We had the radio on in the car and learned that earlier that evening at the world famous Millrose Games in New York City's Madison Square Garden, someone had race-walked the mile in under six minutes to set a world record.

"You mean some guy *walked* the mile in under six minutes and you *ran* it in 6:34?" my father said. He was quite perplexed.

"I guess so," I said, feeling humiliated.

"I'll bet the track at Madison Square Garden is a lot faster than the track where you ran tonight," he said.

I nodded in agreement. "And I bet that guy didn't go to eight classes during the day," I said and broke out into a big smile.

That's the way my father was. He would find something positive in just about anything I did. He would marvel at my foul balls even when I struck out in little league, and he always praised how I could dribble the basketball— even in games when I didn't score and missed all five of my shots.

I try very hard as a teacher and parent to be as positive as he was. I often remind my students when they do poorly on a test that they still have a good chance of getting into Harvard one day, despite getting only 6 out of 10 right on the spelling quiz. I remind my very nervous female cross-country runners that one day they will probably end up marrying a nice guy and having two kids, a great career, a big house with a dog, and wonderful vacations in the Caribbean—and how they run that day at the meet probably won't make a difference one way or the other. They usually laugh, and it calms them down.

Progress with a smile. My fellow not-so-hot distance runner friends became known as the "Loads" on our freshmen track team. The varsity distance runners would go out for eight-mile distance runs. The middle group would run five miles, and the Loads would run three miles. Usually this meant we would run around in the woods and play games with sticks and tennis balls, and when we got back to the school we would always be covered with mud and leaves. The other groups would always be back long before us.

The Loads, all ten of us, would run around and sing songs. We made up a song called the "Load Song," with lyrics sung to the tune of "Ballad of the Green Berets," which was from a very lame John Wayne movie about the Vietnam War. Every time we would go out for a run we would begin singing the "Load Song":

Grubby sweat upon his face.
Kick him out of the human race.
He is slow as any load,
Slower than a starving toad.

They go out to run ten miles.
They are met by many smiles,
But they know what's behind those smiles—
They are smiling at their running styles.

All these loads don't know when to quit.
They are just not physically fit.
But they will try to win today,
And end up last anyway.

When they leave the track for good,
The other runners will say, "Thought they never would."
Will they be missed about the track?
We doubt that that will be a fact.

Our coach, a fun-loving priest named Father Sean who used to smoke cigarettes all through practice, even referred to us as the Loads.

I think the main reason we kept coming to practice was because we were having so much fun, and in the process we all started to get better. My first mile in December of my freshmen year, I ran 6:34, but in May of my freshmen year, I was running the half-mile in 2:33 and the mile in 5:39. I had improved about one minute in five months. At this rate, I was destined to be a world record holder in about a year.

Through my high school career I continued improving, and when I was a senior I was the top runner on the team with a best time in the mile of 4:28. I also owned the school record in the two-mile at 9:37. My fellow Loads all had improved. One of them ended up running 1:59 for the half-mile, and another ran the 440 yard run in just over 50 seconds. Most importantly, we were still laughing, having fun and playing jokes on each other. We never lost that ability to be playful, and our coaches were playful right along with us. It was a wonderful atmosphere of fun. Our cross-country team was ranked 23rd in New York State that year, but if there had been a ranking for a team that had fun, then we would have been number one.

Having fun at school. If having fun can work in sports, why can't it work in schools? It can. A playful attitude can help teachers and kids alike.

After seven years as a high school English teacher, I took a job teaching seventh grade English at Bethlehem Central Middle School near Albany, New York. I had not been adequately prepared for the change, and I came out of that school after my first week looking like a returned prisoner of war. These seventh graders were wild. They had so much energy. The blood and the hormones were just shooting through them.

The year before, I had taught English literature to twelfth graders who were applying to Brown and Harvard. Now I was trying to get 25 seventh graders to all sit down at once. I had more kids with exploding pens that year than in my previous seven years combined.

So I didn't feel much like laughing in the faculty room between classes, but again, as the year progressed, I began to gain the upper hand and learn how to teach seventh grade. They are a very different beast than twelfth graders. I began to reach them when I remembered what it was like being in seventh grade, and I remembered the things that meant a lot to me then. As a seventh grader, I couldn't stay in my seat for very long. Remembering that, I began teaching in 10 to 15 minute blocks. I got the students moving around the room as much as possible. We began to have fun, and that's when I began to relax.

Once I began to relax at work, I began to find all the other coworkers with similar philosophies. We began to eat together at lunch and those lunches became legendary. One day we were laughing so much that a teacher in a classroom next door had to come in and ask us to be quiet. The laughter was a great way to bond, and we have remained strong friends to this day. The laughter at lunch would also follow us down the hall and back to our classrooms. Our students always enjoyed the class after lunch when we were all so relaxed, and the laughter would also energize us.

One thing I have discovered is that one person can't make a school a fun place to work. It must start with teachers who are comfortable having fun. The principal can encourage it, but he or she can't implement it. It must be natural, not forced.

The same thing applies to a teacher's classroom. A teacher can do what feels natural, adding humor in small ways that seem comfortable. For example, after teaching the novel *Deliverance*, I gave my students a 15-minute essay to write, and just as they began writing, I turned on the song "Dueling Banjos" from the movie. They had a good laugh, shook their heads, and continued writing their essays. But they wrote with smiles on their faces.

When we're doing something tedious in class, like a grammar lesson or learning how to write a research paper, I'm the first to admit that the work can be dull. But I also want students to know that not everything in our lives is going to be fun. If we can acknowledge our boredom, then we can begin to deal with it.

In my early years as a teacher, I used to give all that "blah, blah, blah" about how students needed to return books they had borrowed from me: "And if I don't get them by June, then I'll send a note home to your parents and blah, blah, blah!"

You know the speech. The students also knew the speech, and most of them were yawning and thinking about something else. Now I tell my seventh graders about my friend Vinny who lives in the closet. Vinny is my link to the underworld. He does jobs for me that I don't want to do. He gets back books that students have borrowed and not returned. Vinny is the person who cleans up my "situations."

When I talk about Vinny, my classes perk up. "What does Vinny look like?" one student will ask.

"I don't really know," I say, "because if I look at Vinny for too long, he gets angry. And I really don't want to make Vinny angry."

"How can Vinny live in that little closet?"

"He built a loft."

The questions go on and on, and when a student does owe me a book, I will remind that person, "You need to get that book back to me. We don't want a *situation*, and I don't want to send Vinny to your house."

I usually get the book back the next day, and sometimes the student will tell the class, "Vinny came over at two in the morning and *made* me give the book back."

Fun with Bruno Baker. Being playful can even translate into a lesson. As a prelude to our journalism unit, I tell my middle school students early in the school year about my friend Bruno Baker, a supposed film director I went to high school with, who attended UCLA Film School. I mention that he directed an independent film called *Psycho Killer*, which won an award at the Sundance Film Festival.

"I've seen that movie," some student will always say.

"That movie was rated R," I'll tell the student. "You're too young to have seen it."

"But it was a good movie."

I'll tell the class that Bruno usually likes to visit during the school year. "He's a bit of a character," I tell them, "and if he's able to stop by for a visit, he usually likes to role-play a press conference." I mention that before he got into film directing he used to be an actor and had numerous small parts in many popular films such as *E.T. the Extra-Terrestrial* and *Return of the Jedi*.

As the school year continues, I'll periodically drop reminders about Bruno. "Did anyone watch Conan O'Brien last night?"

My students will all sit there and shake their heads.

"Oh, yeah, that's right," I'll say. "That show's on too late. Of course you didn't watch it. But if you had, then you would have seen my friend Bruno Baker. He was a guest and he was really funny!"

As we get closer to our journalism unit, I keep my classes posted on how I've been trying to contact Bruno. "I called his apartment in New York last night," I'll say, "but his maid mentioned he was in Malibu. So I called Malibu and his maid out there said he was attending a film festival in Paris. I'll try back next week." I'll shake my head. "These Hollywood types!"

Now I start getting a few more students who claim to have seen *Psycho Killer.*

"Did you call Bruno again?" a student will ask.

"Is he back from Paris?" another will inquire.

Finally, after we have begun our journalism unit, I inform all my classes that I finally got a commitment from Bruno and that he will indeed visit later in the week. "He's coming home for Mother's Day this weekend," I'll tell the classes. "He's a good son. He grew up on Adams Place right near the school here."

I usually have one student who will say, "I live on Adams Place, and I think I know who his mom is."

When the magical day finally arrives, about half the kids are very excited. Twenty-five percent of them don't believe he's coming. They don't even think there is a Bruno Baker. "I did a Google search," one student said a few years ago, "and there was nothing for Bruno Baker or *Psycho Killer.*" The remaining 25 percent aren't quite sure what to believe, but they like all the excitement anyway.

On the day of Bruno's visit, I tell the first period class that he is taking a limousine from New York City and will be here soon. While we wait, I explain that Mr. Baker wants to have a press conference. We go over the procedure for press conferences and talk about press conferences that have been televised. I also talk about my experiences at a few of the press conferences I've attended as a journalist. All we need then is Bruno Baker. The tension builds.

Bruno arrives. Finally the door opens and a teacher, looking very concerned, enters. "Mr. Rightmyer," the teacher will say, "there's a limousine in front of the school and a Mr. Baker is here to see you."

I nod my head. "Yeah, I've been expecting him. Send him down."

"Well, the main office people would like you to meet him and walk down with him."

I'll roll my eyes. "All right! Is there any way you could watch my class for me till I get back?"

The teacher agrees, and I tell the class I'll be right back. Some students are sitting very upright, both nervous and excited. Others are just rolling their eyes and laughing, and there are a few students who keep checking everyone's faces because they don't know how to react.

This is when I go into my Clark Kent mode and rush to an already chosen hideout and quickly change into my Bruno Baker costume. Bruno has long black hair that falls to his shoulders. He wears dark sunglasses, a black leather jacket over a white T-shirt, and a pair of jeans. After my quick change, I go back to the class-room and back in so that the first thing my students see is Baker's shoulder length hair. Then I turn around, and the room erupts into laughter.

"You're Mr. Rightmyer," someone will scream.

"I knew there was no Bruno Baker," another student will laugh.

"You thought you knew his mother," another student will say.

Now my real work takes place. Without laughing, I must stay in the role of Bruno and begin the press conference. "I called you all here today because I'm not a very happy camper," I'll begin. "As you know, I am Bruno Baker, award-winning film director, and I'm proud of my body of work. I not only make good movies, but my movies are works of art. Still, I haven't forgotten you, the little people. I came back to this little town where I grew up to bring you a present and to help the people who gave me my start, and I've been treated like garbage."

I pause at this point. "I suggest you reporters get your notebooks out and start writing down what I'm saying." Now the students realize we're still in a classroom and having a press conference. "Like I said, I came back to this little backwater town to say thanks and to help you, and I can't believe the way I've been treated. My plan is to make the sequel to the movie *Psycho Killer*, titled *Son of Psycho Killer*, and to film it in this town. I wanted to make about half the film at this middle school, but your principal won't let me film here. He doesn't want an R-rated movie being filmed at his middle school."

I go on and on for a few more minutes about how much money the movie will generate for the area, and I talk about some of the famous stars who have committed to be in the film. Then I open the floor for questions.

Each student, when called upon, stands up, asks a question, and then is allowed a follow-up question. "Do you think, Mr. Baker, that the people here will like that you called the town a 'backwater' town?"

I shrug my shoulders. "I call it the way I see it. I don't see vacation destinations to this place, but I want to give back to my roots. I want to help this town by making *Son of Psycho Killer* here. I can make it anywhere I want in the world, but I want to give back to the place where I started."

As the press conference continues, I get some questions like "Aren't you Mr. Rightmyer?" But I always remain in the role of Baker. I answer questions like this by saying, "I don't know what you're talking about, but we have a serious problem going on, and that's what this principal of your middle school is doing to me and the entire community."

As any actor will tell you, it's a lot of fun being another person, and I love acting as Bruno Baker. I love being irreverent, and I love saying things I would never have the courage to say as myself. Bruno always stops the press conference with about 15 minutes of class time left, giving me enough time to quickly go and change back into Mr. Rightmyer.

When I return to the class, a few students will yell, "You're Bruno Baker."

I will shake my head. "No, I'm not, but I did overhear what he was saying, and what I'd like you to do now is write up your straight news article about what you heard at the press conference."

It's important for me to be serious and stick to my role as a classroom teacher for the last part of class. I quickly calm the students down and get them back on task—writing their articles.

I want students to know that what happened to them is what can happen at a press conference. I tell them about a time I attended a press conference held by a professional football player who spent much of the conference making fun of both our town and newspaper reporters. "But I still had to go back to that paper and write a straight news article about what he said, and I could not give my opinion," I said.

When the class ends, I know my students have had a good time, have done some laughing, have experienced something of what it feels like to be at a real press conference, and have started writing a news article. Many of them will remember this class period more than just about any other during the entire school year.

The power of fun. One of my most enjoyable times of the year occurs for two weeks in August when I am one of the directors of the Step Up Program. The Step Up Program began in 1990 as a way to reach incoming sixth grade students who were considered at-risk by their elementary teachers and principals. It was the brainchild of my school's fifth grade teacher Mary Capobianco, who was tired of seeing a core of kids fall through the cracks when they went from elementary school to the much larger middle school. Mary wrote up a plan to start a two-week summer program to give these kids a boost and help their self-esteem before they entered middle school. She put a call out to any middle school teachers who would want to help implement the program. I responded, along with a sixth grade science teacher and a sixth grade physical education teacher, and we spent two days talking about the goals of the program and how we could carry it out.

We had great ideals in the beginning. We were going to have the kids read at least two books, and they were going to complete complex scientific experiments and we would get them walking up on the high ropes in our physical education Project Adventure area.

It didn't quite turn out that way. We had 22 kids, and half of them were not the quiet, insecure kids we had been expecting. They tended more towards being bullies—a type of at-risk student, but not the type we intended for the program. These class clowns had a feast in the first few days making fun of the more appropriately selected quiet, at-risk students.

"The opposite of what we want is happening in this program," Mary said. "We wanted to bring in shy kids to meet other shy kids and show them what the school will be like and have them learn their way around the building, and instead we're bringing these insecure kids in here and making them more insecure by the minute."

The four of us kept tweaking the program. "There's no way they can read two books," I said. "Maybe we can read part of one book."

"I can't bring them up on the high ropes until they trust each other and learn how to work together," said our P.E. teacher, Bob.

"They don't listen," said our science teacher, Alexia. "We can't do any experiments if they don't listen. Someone will get hurt."

We decided to spend the rest of the first week teaching them how to listen and follow directions. We corrected bad behavior whenever it happened and praised any type of good behavior we saw. For a few days it felt more like a Scared Straight Program put on by hardened convicts, but what got us through was how well the four of us worked together.

When all the kids went home at 3:00 we would sit in front of the school, eat popsicles and laugh about what a miserable day it had been. There was a lot of gallows humor going on.

There clearly was positive growth with the kids in the second week. They got along better and picked on each other much less. The four teachers also began to laugh more, especially during the day. We were feeling much more relaxed, and we noticed that the kids seemed to enjoy watching us joke with each other.

"Maybe I'll try them on the high ropes after all," Bob said.

Bob not only tried them, but at least 75 percent of the kids climbed the 30 feet up the tree and walked across the bridge, cheering for each other and encouraging the reluctant climbers.

The two-week program, which had started out so miserably, became one of the best educational experiences of my life. On the last day, we had a graduation ceremony, and we gave an award to each student. Mostly they were wacky awards, such as "The Person with the Greatest Last Name in the World," which went to a girl who also had the name of Rightmyer. The kids received their awards with much laughter, and as they were leaving were saying things like, "I can't wait for school to start in two weeks."

We received many compliments from the parents and many thank-you letters. "My son has never liked school," one parent wrote, "but after a few days at the Step Up Program he looked forward to coming and wanted to get there early and stay late. He had a lot of fun and said the teachers were very funny. Thank you for giving him the confidence to go to the "BIG" middle school. He's now looking forward to it, and in the beginning of the summer he was dreading it."

The four of us have continued the Step Up Program every summer since 1990. We've added a few new teachers, but we've also kept the fun in the program. I often tell my friends that those two weeks are my favorite two weeks of the year. I don't have to worry about correcting. There is no test to give at the end. All I'm doing is working with kids, having fun with them, teaching them some important skills they'll need to be successful at the middle school, and enjoying my time with my peers. I've often wished that my regular school year could be as much fun as the Step Up Program.

Being Playful Can Lead to SUCCESS

At the middle school where I teach, I sometimes see kids wandering around the hallway with dazed, zombie-like expressions. Many of them tell me how boring school is, and when I ask them what they do after school, they usually say, "Hang around with my friends, play video games, or watch TV."

They usually say this with little or no expression, and I want to open up their craniums and pour some life in there. I hate to see young people so aimless and bored. Maybe that's why I love to coach the high school girls' cross-country team. These girls don't look bored.

"We are all here for a spell; get all the good laughs you can."

– Will Rogers

Girls and sports. All the research shows that upon entering middle schools, many girls suffer a loss of self-esteem. Their scores drop in math and science, and many of them stop participating in class discussions. Many become followers, content to let the more dominant male adolescents lead.

Research shows that girls who do best during this troubling time period are the ones involved in sports. Numerous studies have found that participation in sports builds self-confidence, provides valuable lessons in self-discipline, and helps develop skills to handle competitive situations.

We have come a long way from the days when people made fun of girls who participated in sports and called them names. I remember interviewing Joan Benoit Samuelson, the 1984 Olympic marathon gold medalist, who told me how much she loved to run in the early 1970s when she was in high school. "But where I lived in Maine, there were no girls who ran," she said. "Still, I'd go out on these country roads and just run and run, and it felt so good, but I remember when I'd hear a car coming down the road I'd stop and walk or sometimes pick some wildflowers along the side of the road because people would think I was so strange to be out running alone for no reason."

Today if you drive near any upstate New York high school in the fall, you will probably see many girls out running, and they aren't picking wildflowers. The high school girls' cross-country teams in this area are among the best in the country. Believe me, these athletes have no self-esteem problem. The girls are strong because they work hard. They seem never to have heard the statement that girls can't do something, and if they have heard it, they certainly know it's not true.

And the girls succeed despite little press coverage from the area newspapers. The football and soccer teams get the most attention, but the girls know how good they are. They run for many of the same reasons that Joan Benoit Samuelson ran—because it just feels so good.

I always get back a lot when I cheer on those runners, the ones at the front of the pack and the ones who stagger to the finish line. I love watching these high school girls take a risk and gain some confidence.

The girls do well in competitions, and I believe one of the reasons is our sense of playfulness. Our teams have fun. While other teams sometimes look serious and dour faced at meets, we always looked pretty relaxed and carefree. We laugh at practice, at meets, and on the bus rides. We work hard and always want to do our best, but I have always tried to remind the girls that what's really important is not so much what we accomplish but how we accomplish it.

Practice, practice, practice. Every year, we begin practice in the middle of August, and these are some of my favorite days of the year. Three of our practice days, we meet at an environmental center where there are about 15 miles of trails going through the woods, through fields, by streams. We often see deer and all sorts of birds. It's a relaxed and important part of our training, and it reminds us why we like to run. I stress that what's important is not how fast they complete the run, but that they maintain a steady pace and look around and have fun. Generally, the only noise you will hear when you're out on the trails is the laughter coming from the packs of runners.

After practice, Kim, the other coach, and I wait around and talk and laugh with the girls as they wait for their rides. This is as important as anything we've done during the practice because it is all part of the team-building that's so important for a successful team.

There are some cross-country coaches who actually cut the slowest runners from their teams. "I only want 20 to 25 runners on my squad," a successful coach once told me. "I don't want any of those hanger-on kids. They just get in the way. Most of them are lazy, and I don't want their bad attitudes creeping into the program."

Well, I have a lot of those 'hanger-on' kids, and I have no problem with them. I know a teenage girl takes a big risk when she joins a team that has to run a three-mile race up and down hills twice a week. Part of the fun of coaching is letting girls who have never been athletic join the team. One year, a girl on the team normally finished last in every race, but as she came to the finish line I would always cheer her on and she would smile and smile. Once I asked her why she always smiled when I cheered for her and she said,

"Mr. Rightmyer, until this year, I've never been on a sports team, ever, so when you cheer for me it makes me feel so good. No one ever cheered for me in my life."

Deciding to run for glory. One of the best experiences of my teaching and coaching career happened in 2004 when I was coaching at Bethlehem Central High School. We heard that Nike was going to sponsor a national high school cross-country championship race, the Nike Team Nationals, and we decided to try to participate. But first we had to become nationally ranked, and that meant competing in the Great American Cross Country Festival in Cary, North Carolina.

In Cary, we piled the girls into a van we had rented and drove out to the course where they would race the next day. We had the radio cranked up and the girls were singing along and laughing, and it felt like the last day of school. But as we pulled into the parking lot where the college races were going on and where their race would go on the next day, a deathly silence invaded the van.

"I've never seen so many people at a cross-country race before," Emily said.

I bought a program and we walked around for awhile looking at all the different schools—both high school and college teams. We all knew that Saratoga, a team from our own league, would be here. That team was currently the number one team in the country, but the number two team in the country, Smoky Hill from Colorado, was also in our race, along with other top 20 teams from California, Texas, Florida, Maryland—just about everywhere.

Just before we began jogging the course, I got the girls together and tried to give them a pep talk. "What a great opportunity we have here," I told them. "You'll remember this for the rest of your life. Just remember that this course is the same length as every other 3.1 mile course we've run all year." I was trying to give my emotional pep talk like the one Gene Hackman gives in the movie *Hoosiers,* but my team wasn't ready for any of that. I can sense when I'm losing my audience, so all I ended up saying was, "Let's get out on the course and jog it and talk about some strategy."

As we jogged the course there was little of the usual joking and laughing. I could tell the girls were more uptight than normal, and I was hearing a lot of complaints.

"It's so muggy."

"This course is really wet and muddy."

"All those teams in our race look so good."

"Mr. Rightmyer, do you think we're gonna finish last?"

On the van ride back to the hotel I told the girls to relax for a few hours, take a shower and meet back in the lobby around 5:30 for dinner. Then Kim and I walked across the street to this enormous mall, hoping to find a pasta place where we could eat dinner.

"I've never seen them so tense," Kim said.

"I think we're tense, too," I said.

"I think they can do really well, as long as they relax and just go out there and do it."

We found an Italian restaurant and made reservations. The bartender told us it was karaoke night. "Every Friday night Frankie plays here. He's a singer and he likes to get patrons up and get them dancing and singing with him. He's got quite a local following, but I'm not sure if your girls will like him. He plays a lot of old songs."

Frankie. Old songs. Karaoke. Dancing. Kim and I smiled. "What time does he start ?" I asked.

"I'm here to entertain you." The waiters and even the owner of
the restaurant came out to greet us when we arrived with the girls
later. "I hear you're running in a big race tomorrow," the owner
said. "I want to wish you good luck. We hope our food helps you
run your best."

The girls were all smiles. We ordered and were about halfway
through our meal when we heard a short Italian man speak into a
microphone. "Hello, ladies and gentlemen. My name is Frankie,
and I'm here to entertain you." Then he started singing "Volare."
He had all the typical wedding singer moves, shifting the microphone from one hand to another, walking around the dinner
patrons, putting his hand around their shoulders and singing to
them.

The girls on the team shifted their eyes back and forth at each
other. Should they laugh? Should they hide?

It took only a few songs before Frankie wandered over to the
girls. "And what's your name?" he asked one of my tiny ninth grade
runners.

"Kristin," she said, turning red.

"And where are you from, Kristin?"

"New York," she said, and the entire team laughed and cheered.

"I'm from New York," Frankie said. "New York's my favorite
place. If you can make it there, you can make it anywhere." And
then Frankie immediately began singing "New York, New York."
Four or five of the girls jumped up with him and began singing and
dancing right along with him, and for the next 45 minutes the team
became the star of the show. They told him they were running in a
championship high school cross-country race the next morning.

"And we're the 17th best cross-country team in the country,"
one of the girls said. By now, the entire restaurant was cheering
them on.

On our walk back to the hotel, all the girls talked about was
Frankie, his songs, and those cheers. It had been the perfect
night. The team had stayed relaxed, laughed, and had a good
time.

The day of the race. We had a quick meeting in one of the
rooms when we got back. I went through our itinerary and told
the girls what starting box we would be running in.

"I can't believe we're box 27," Taylor said. "That's a lot of
boxes. There are some great teams here."

"We got the best box," I told them. "Box 27 is perfect. All you
have to do is run straight ahead, and you'll get off to a good start.
I saw all the boxes today and 27 is the best."

"Really?" Emily said.

The truth is that I hadn't even noticed where box 27 was.
Whenever the girls complain about something just before they
run, I've learned to turn that complaint around and make it into
a positive. "It's too hot today," a runner will say, and I'll respond,
"Isn't that great! We always run well in the heat."

On the ride to the course the next morning, I didn't hear any
complaints. The girls were somewhat quiet, but I could tell they
were ready to run. We found box 27 about 15 minutes before the
race. "It really is a great box," Roxanne said.

"Didn't I tell you that?" I said, giving a quick glance to Kim,
who was laughing and trying not to be seen.

The race is on. A few minutes before the race, the announcer said, "And now the featured girls' race of the day, the Nike Race of Champions." Kim and I told the girls we would be out on the trails cheering them on. As we jogged away we took a quick look back to see the 27 teams and over 200 runners standing on the line ready for the gun to go off. I could still hear the announcer say, "And the main event today in this race will be a battle between New York's Saratoga High School, ranked number one in the nation, and Smoky Hill from Colorado, ranked number 2 in the nation."

I looked at Kim and said, "I can't believe we're here."

And then the gun sounded and the runners took off. I stared down the trail with all the other spectators, and I could barely make out the flashing lights of the pace car and a few runners close behind it. I kept reminding myself that we came to this meet to run with the best. It's a great experience for these kids, no matter what happens.

As the race neared its end, the top few runners came sprinting by, and I kept counting them. We saw Emily finish 22nd, Kristin 32nd, Roxanne 34th, Claire 55th, Megan 77th, Carly 87th and Taylor 93rd.

Kim and I were busy hugging all the girls when a race official walked through the area and announced, "Would the following teams please report to the award stand?" He named five teams, and one of them was us.

When we arrived, the announcer said, "Ladies and gentlemen, we have the official results in for the Nike Race of Champions, and defending their title with a team score of 26 points is Saratoga High School, currently ranked number one in the nation."

There was some applause from the crowd and the seven runners from Saratoga walked up and stood on the stand reserved for the number one team. The girls were smiling, but they also looked relieved that the race was over and once again they had won. Some of the Saratoga parents stood around and took a few pictures of the team. It was all a pleasant sight, somewhat reserved and quite professional looking.

Then the announcer picked up the microphone and said, "And in second place, also from New York, is Bethlehem High School with 154 points."

And that's when mass hysteria set in. We all started screaming and jumping around. "We beat the number two ranked team in the country," I said to Kim. Everybody was hugging each other. Some parents were crying. Most of the girls were crying. We were carrying on to the point that the announcer had to ask the girls to please come up on the award stand and get their medals and plaque.

All seven girls jumped up on the stand, and then they yelled for all of us to join them. We all jumped up with them—the junior varsity runners, the coaches, the parents. There were 20 of us up on the award stand with the winners as people cheered and took pictures. Even the Saratoga coaches were laughing at how we were carrying on.

We didn't care how foolish we looked. This was a team that had worked hard, played hard, and laughed hard, and the team members had fulfilled their dream of placing in the top five. Actually, they had gone well beyond their dream. They had become the surprise of the meet, defeating the number two ranked team in the country.

Hometown heroes. On the flight home, one of the parents had the pilot announce shortly after takeoff, "Ladies and gentlemen, we would like to announce that we have a special group on board today's flight. The Bethlehem girls' cross-country team is flying with us, and this afternoon they finished second at the Great American Cross-country Meet, where they defeated the number two ranked team in the country."

The girls all began cheering, and when we arrived back home at the airport, many of the parents who had not attended met us at the gate. They were holding balloons, carrying posters and cheering us as we marched from the plane. The whole weekend was one of the most marvelous experiences I've ever been part of.

And did we get invited to that Nike National High School Championship Race? We did. The eight girls who attended had perhaps the best weekend of their lives. They received an all-expense paid three-day trip from Albany, New York, to Portland, Oregon, and brand new racing shoes, shorts, singlets, and warm-up suits. They also met many Olympians, toured the Nike compound, and were treated like world-class athletes.

Their favorite event during that weekend was the night before the race when the people at Nike gave all the teams non-permanent markers and told the runners to decorate the white vans the teams would be using to get to the meet early the next morning. The Bethlehem girls' team was out there for over 45 minutes, and the girls covered every inch of that van with pictures and slogans. It was the perfect way for our team to diffuse all the tension of running in a national high school cross-country race clear across the country.

And as that Bethlehem girls' team was lined up with 19 other great teams from all over the country, I felt so proud of what they had accomplished. No, they didn't win the race, but they did finish 13th out of the 20 best girls' teams in the nation. I must say that our van had the funniest slogans and pictures, and I don't think any team in Portland that weekend had as much fun as they did.

Nothing Funny About DISCIPLINE

You can choose your attitude in the classroom. You can make connections. You can create a relaxed atmosphere that welcomes humor. All that, however, can take you only so far. To succeed, every teacher must deal with the very serious matter of discipline.

According to John O'Neil in an article called "Discipline Zingers" (*NEA Today, January, 2004*), teachers and support professionals interviewed by *NEA Today* said that "kids today have the same needs as always—to be accepted, competent, respected—but they seem needier than ever." That neediness, they speculate, explains why so many of today's students act out and are so disruptive.

Ask teachers out in the trenches today and they will tell you that today's students are less respectful of authority and harder to discipline than students of past years. They will also tell you that the problem is not that students' behavior is more difficult to manage; the real problem is the increased *number* of students displaying unacceptable or inappropriate behavior.

Many disruptive kids come from one-parent families, and some are in foster care. Some have never met their fathers. Many have poor role models, from family members to movie stars, pop stars and sports celebrities. Many of them have parents who are absent, uninvolved, or too busy to provide structure and guidance in their children's lives. Many children return to empty homes after school. When they go to school, many of them face overcrowded and impersonal environments with curriculums that have no bearing on their lives. It's no wonder many of them are bored, angry and willing to act out in class.

> "Humor keeps you in the present. It is very difficult to laugh and be disassociated with the people around you. In that one moment together you have unity and a new chance."
>
> – Alexis Driscoll

Creating boundaries for students. Being able to skillfully handle classroom discipline problems is one of the most important skills any teacher can develop—and not having that skill is one of the reasons many new teachers end up leaving the profession.

As a teacher for over 28 years, I've learned that all students, especially the most needy ones, want to know where the boundaries are. Students want structure, even though most of them will say they don't, especially those students who have no structure in their home lives.

If a student is being unruly, we can't look the other way and hope the student will stop. We can create something big out of a little problem, or we can deflate what could be enormous and use it as a way to connect with a student.

As teachers, we need to create a safe environment where all students feel relaxed and willing to take necessary academic risks. We can't be a friend or a buddy to students, especially to our most needy students. We also can't be so strict that our students have little or no chit-chat time. This type of classroom atmosphere only instills an adversarial relationship between the teachers and the students.

There have been many studies about classroom management procedures. Some of the effective procedures that have worked well for me are these:

1. Lay the groundwork with effective rules and procedures.

For rules and procedures to be effective, they must be established the very first day of class. That's the day I hand out my course curriculum, which includes what I hope to accomplish as a teacher, what we will be studying during the school year, and how I expect my students to behave. I take some time to point out some of the posters in my room, one about classroom behavior and another about put-downs. I always ask my students if they have any other classroom rules they feel should be included on the poster. I always get some student who will say, "There should be no homework."

And I say, "That's not a behavior, but I promise I won't give any homework that's a waste of your time."

Some classroom management programs include the following guidelines, which have worked well for me:

- State the rules in a positive fashion.
- Use age-appropriate, kid-friendly language.
- Limit the number of rules.
- Post them prominently in the classroom.
- Have students discuss the rules, rehearse them, and demonstrate they understand them.

If classroom behavior problems persist into the year, it's never too late to re-establish why there are rules and procedures all students are expected to follow. I've had to do this on numerous occasions with certain classes, and I try to do it as positively as I can. It's never a good idea to put down students with statements like, "Why can't you follow these simple rules?" or "What's wrong with you?" or "How many times have I told you to copy down the homework when you first walk into class?" I might *think* these thoughts, but I keep them to myself. I'm the professional. I need to model good classroom behavior if I expect my students to do the same.

2. Create a supportive classroom climate. Students need to feel safe, respected and wanted if they're ever going to get to the point where real learning will take place. As teachers, we need to create a classroom environment that fosters positive values, where we treat each other with respect and where we respect everyone's right to learn.

In my classroom, I want all my students to feel relaxed, to laugh, to want to take a risk with their reading and their writing. I want a classroom that's filled with excited learners who want to participate in class activities, rather than bored passive viewers who keep checking the wall clock for when they can leave.

If I show passion in my teaching, and if I treat all my students with respect, then I will have helped to create a classroom that's positive and supportive for everyone.

3. Work on relationships with kids and with parents. A good friend who was a New York City police officer told me that a big part of being a good cop was forming relationships with the people on his beat—the residents, the store-owners, the kids, and the troublemakers.

"Once people know you care about them, they start to care about you," he said, "and when the people I'm trying to protect care about me, then we're all going to benefit."

The same can be said of teachers. If you want to be a teacher, but you're afraid of connecting with people, then let me tell you, you're in the wrong profession. The best teachers form positive relationships with the students and their parents, and one of the best ways to make a connection with students is to take the time to notice them and show an interest in *their* interests. Parents know you care when you return their phone calls or e-mail messages. They also know you care when you show that you are also interested in their child's development as a student.

A great way to show students you care is to catch them being good. Instead of calling home only when a student is doing poorly or when something bad has happened, I try to call home when the child has done well on a test, given an excellent oral presentation, done a nice job helping another student, or perhaps even done a favor for me. One of the great things about e-mail is that I can easily contact parents with positive messages about their children, and I can also do this on my teacher's web site.

When I think of my favorite teachers, they were clearly the ones who formed relationships with me. They knew my name, knew what my interests were, and were present at games, concerts, and plays. They were also the ones who often gave encouragement or good-natured criticism. Brother Smith used to get on my case all the time about how I was such a big Boston Red Sox fan. "If you keep rooting for them," he would say, "you're going to die at an early age." What I liked about him was that he *knew* I was a Red Sox fan.

4. "Work the room," handling disruptions as quietly as possible.

Even in the best classrooms, kids misbehave. The best way to deal with these disruptions is quickly, before they have a chance to escalate. I try to never make a big deal out of misbehavior, since I know that it's usually a student's way of getting some attention.

Prevention begins with awareness. As teachers, we need to learn how to see all areas of the room. It's been my experience that you can do this only if you're relaxed.

I also try not to take discipline problems personally. If I'm talking and some student is laughing or talking in another part of the room, I'll often stop and say, "Sam, you should listen to this because it might change your life." The line usually gets a few laughs, and then I'm able to continue the lesson.

I make a point never to get too upset over misbehavior. I remind myself that misbehavior usually happens when a student is undergoing some family or friend issue. When a student has been acting poorly, I'll usually ask, "Is everything okay? Why are you giving me and the class such a hard time? What are we doing to you?" This usually calms a student down and, I hope, shows him that I really do care not only about his behavior, but also about him.

5. Be flexible. I learned a long time ago that if I was going to survive as a teacher, I needed to be flexible. There are some days when my students just aren't capable of sitting down, taking notes and listening to a lecture, and there are other days when I can't let them work together in groups because of their high energy. As a veteran teacher, I've learned to quickly change gears and try something different when necessary. The time of day matters a lot, also. My classes are much more squirrelly late in the day than they are during first period. I need to adjust my lessons accordingly.

And it's okay to stop every so often when something is not working and ask the class, "What's going on here? Why is everyone so noisy today? We have a lot that we have to get through and this isn't helping." What I really want to say is "Stop busting my ass!" When I'm honest with the class about how they're driving me crazy, I've often found out some interesting things:

"I've got a big game this afternoon and I'm nervous about it."

"I'm worried about getting my report card tomorrow."

"I have too many tests coming up this week. I just can't concentrate."

When classes are honest with me, I'll sometimes negotiate with them. "Okay, tell you what," I'll say. "Because you're all stressed about too many tests tomorrow, I'll drop the quiz I'd planned for tomorrow and give it to you next Tuesday."

Sometimes when the classes are completely out of it, I'll take the last ten minutes and play a game of trivia. It's fun. It gets them back on task, and it's a great way to sneak in a little review, especially when the trivia questions are about information we've covered for the week.

What about bullying? A few years ago, I was contacted by Andrew, a high school senior, who asked me if he could intern for me at the middle school for the second half of the school year. I had taught Andrew five years earlier when he was in seventh grade, and I remembered him as creative and a little bit eccentric. "I'd love to be your mentor," I told him, after thinking about it for a nanosecond.

From March through June, Andrew came in just about every afternoon from noon until 3:00 p.m. He photocopied papers, ran errands, and did computer research. I always tried to involve him in every class I taught. It was a wonderful experience to work with him on a daily basis. He was able to see education a bit through the eyes of a teacher, and I was able to see the classroom a bit through his eyes. We both came away wiser because of the work.

My students took to Andrew right away. He wasn't a student; he wasn't quite a student teacher; and he definitely was not the teacher. My classes seemed to think of him as one of them, yet a bit wiser. They referred to him as Dr. Andrew, and they valued his input, especially in the areas of film and journalism.

Andrew has no plans to be a teacher, even though he would make an excellent one. He wanted to do his internship with me because he wanted to explore an issue that was a major concern for him—bullying. I was a bit shocked when he told me so during his first week.

"Yeah, it's really bad, Mr. Rightmyer," he said, "and most teachers aren't even aware of it."

I suspected that he was right. I make a point of standing in the hallway every morning before homeroom with the intention of stopping bullying and making sure there are no student fights in the hallway, but there are so many students. It would be impossible for a teacher to be everywhere. I'm there to see the flagrant stuff, but there's no way I can pick up on the sneaky mean stuff that goes on under the radar.

"The bullying is a lot more subtle at the high school, but it's very obvious at the middle school," said Andrew. "For my internship, I want to write a paper on bullying, and I want to walk the hallways at the middle school and watch for it in classes and talk to some students."

Andrew's research on bullying. Andrew found a 2005 UCLA Graduate School of Education Study taken in two ethnically diverse urban schools in Los Angeles. It found that 46% of the sixth graders had been bullied at least once in the course of a school week. The National Association of School Psychologists says that five million children are bullied each year, and 160,000 students skip school each day because they're afraid of bullies. Andrew also found that most students believe teachers ignore the problem of bullying.

Andrew told me that he had been the recipient of bullying throughout his school years. "I'm a geek," he'd shrug. "I'm not into sports, and I like comic books." What helped him through the years was finding similar friends, both male and female. "At the high school, especially after ninth grade, people just seem to be more accepting. But it was really bad in middle school," he said.

In his research, Andrew found that schools are trying a variety of programs to stop widespread bullying, such as zero tolerance, bullying courts set up by fellow students, "snitch" programs that encourage students to tattle on their fellow student bullies, student questionnaires about bullying in the school, and a program called "Don't Laugh At Me," founded by Peter Yarrow of the singing group Peter, Paul and Mary. It involves music, videos and classroom activities to sensitize students to the painful effects of bullying behaviors. There are four essential aspects to this program:

1. The first focus is on students learning to express their feelings openly in the classroom.
2. The second focus is on the "Three C's": caring, compassion and cooperation.
3. The third focus is on creative resolutions that avoid violence and put-downs as ways to handle a conflict.
4. The final focus is on learning to appreciate differences and discussing why it is not appropriate to bully students who are different.

There are some excellent programs out there, but what concerns me the most is why there are so many bullies in our schools, and why students and many teachers seem to look the other way when an incident of bullying occurs. According to Andrew, most students just don't want to get involved and help a victim who is being bullied. "I guess they feel it's not their business to help out," said Andrew.

When I hear that, I think back to the classic story, *A Christmas Carol*, by Charles Dickens. When Scrooge is visited by Jacob Marley, his business partner who has been dead for seven years, Scrooge tells his friend, "But you were always a good man of business, Jacob."

Marley is furious to hear this statement and cries, "Business! Mankind was my business. The common welfare was my business; charity, mercy, forbearance, and benevolence, were, all, my business. The dealings of my trade were but a drop of water in the comprehensive ocean of my business!"

How many of us as teachers and students don't get involved because it's none of our business? How many tragedies and school shootings could have been prevented if faculty and students had made it their business to speak up about what a student or a group of students were doing?

Will schools ever be free of bullies? Probably not. But there are many students who bully others out of boredom and unhappiness, and these are the ones we can turn around. There will always be students who are neglected and come from dysfunctional and unhappy families, and we as educators need to reach out to them and be good role models for them. For some children in our classrooms, we may be the only positive role models they meet all day. It's an amazing responsibility, but good teachers have been reaching out for many years now.

Dealing with bullies. As a student, I was surrounded by bullies all the time. I learned at a young age to steer clear of them, but as a teacher I've had to face them head on. I've learned the following when dealing with kids who are chronic behavior problems:

- Deal with them one on one, not in front of the entire class, and certainly not in front of their friends.
- Connecting with them and forming a positive relationship is very important. Is it possible to joke around with a bully? Yes, and most bullies need to laugh. The problem with bullies is that most of them

don't know what is appropriate humor. Pulling a chair out so a student falls might seem funny to the bully, but it's clearly inappropriate. We cannot assume that a bully's close role models demonstrate appropriate humor, and that's where we as teachers need to step in.

- Let them know that you value their opinion and care about them. I had a student once who was always in trouble, but I found out that he knew everything about cars, so that year when I was planning to buy a new car, I asked him what would be the best car for me. Even years after I taught him, he still asks about what car I'm driving.
- Don't preach to them—they've had enough of that through the years. Explain that their behavior is inappropriate and not acceptable, and if they continue it they will be punished, but avoid the big lecture.
- Follow through with the punishment—they will perceive you as weak if you give in—but make sure the punishment is not degrading or humiliating in any way.

In my 28 years of teaching, I have encountered five students who were hard-core bullies. When I had problems with them, I could only deal with them from my position of power: "Don't do that! Go to the principal's office."

Did they become bullies because of something in their genetic makeup? Was it the way they were raised? I'm not a psychologist, so

I don't know. I am a teacher, and my job is to educate and motivate my students. To do that, I must provide a safe environment. I must never put myself or my students in a position where they could be harmed.

FORGIVING and FORGETTING

During my first few anxiety-ridden, insecure years of teaching, I only felt comfortable when my students were quiet and I was doing all the talking. I thought that was good teaching. I had no patience for students who were square pegs and did not fit nicely into the round hole I was attempting to force all my students into. Creativity meant noise, and noise meant I had no control, which meant I was a bad teacher.

Ironically, this attitude created more chaos in my classroom because my students were bored, and I had formed no connection with them. Learning to relax and to laugh in the classroom made me a better teacher. I'm now more comfortable allowing and even encouraging creativity. I have more patience for students who refuse to fit into round holes.

> *"Never discourage anyone who continually makes progress, no matter how slow."*
>
> – Plato

Taking risks with creativity. In the past 20 years, I have become a strong believer in having my students take risks. When they challenge themselves and try something new, that's when they really learn.

Each year, I give students an opportunity to read one of their poems at a poetry reading at a local coffee shop during April, National Poetry Month. About 25 to 40 students usually participate, which is about one-third of all the students I teach. I consider that a pretty high number of risk takers.

Kids who sometimes never shine in an ordinary class often feel like stars for that night. I'm also impressed with the courage my students display in reading an original poem before a crowd of 50 to 100 strangers.

I normally drive home from the poetry reading feeling a bit smug about what an excellent job of teaching and motivating I've done, but there was one year when I drove home wondering if the whole thing was worth it.

The poetry reading takes place at the end of my two-month poetry unit. I make it clear to students that if they choose to read a poem at the reading, they do it for the love of poetry and not because they're going to get any extra credit. I only want serious poets at the reading. Even if they are reading a funny poem, I want them to read the poem well and treat the evening with appropriate decorum.

The poets who attend generally do so for all the right reasons. Many times they dress up more than they do during the school day, and every year I have a few students who wear berets or otherwise dress the way they think a real poet would dress. One year a student put his hand up and said, "Mr. Rightmyer, I was in that coffeehouse last year, and I saw a man wearing a cape."

"Why was he wearing a cape?" I asked.

"I don't know," said the student. "He was just walking around drinking coffee and wearing a cape." He paused while the class laughed at this. "Mr. Rightmyer, if I come to the poetry reading, can I wear a cape?"

I told him he could wear a cape, and a few nights later he did indeed come to the poetry reading wearing a cape.

I begin the poetry night by welcoming the parents, relatives and friends, and then I read the first poem. I want students to know that if they can get up and read one of their original poems in front of their peers, then I can do it also. When I'm finished, I invite five to ten poets to come forward and read their poems.

Each poet walks to the microphone, announces his or her name and poem title, and then reads the poem slowly and—we hope—

loud enough. We've practiced this a few times in class, so usually things go off the way they should.

Then I give the poets an opportunity to answer questions from the audience. This is usually my favorite part of the evening because it gives my students a chance to display their quick wit and intelligence.

The disaster. But one year the question/answer session didn't go quite as planned. The first question from the audience was, "Now that you've studied poetry, written some poems and participated in a poetry reading, do you like poetry more than you did before?" I passed the microphone around from student to student. Most of the students predictably said they enjoyed poetry more than before, but one of my students, a good-natured but usually mischievous seventh grader, said with a smirk, "I always hated poetry. I only read a poem here to get some extra credit."

His remark elicited uproarious laughter from the students and the audience. "We're not getting any extra credit," a student yelled. "Don't you remember Mr. Rightmyer saying that in school this week and even tonight before we all read?"

The clowning kid grabbed the microphone and said, "No extra-credit! Then what am I doing here?"

Now there was more laughter. I was trying to smile, but the smile was gradually wilting a bit into a pained expression. Fortunately a parent quickly raised her hand and I called on her. "Mr. Rightmyer, do you write a lot of poetry?"

Before I could respond, the boy leaned toward the microphone and said, "He writes poetry the way he teaches—bad!" The boy pumped his fist a few times. Some of the students laughed, but the audience was mostly quiet.

In my early days of teaching, I would have prevented the boy from taking the microphone. I may have even said something like, "Let's hear from someone else." But instead I let this boy continue to act this way. I purposely chose not to have a confrontation with the class clown in front of everyone, although I knew he and I would certainly be having a discussion about his behavior, a private discussion, after the poetry reading.

His behavior continued for about 15 minutes. Someone in the audience would ask a question and the boy would grab the microphone and make a sarcastic comment that he thought was hilarious. The only problem was that the audience was no longer laughing, and even most of the students were telling him to be quiet.

After the poetry reading, when I was individually saying goodbye to some students and their parents, the mischievous boy slowly slithered up to me with his mother standing behind him and said rather meekly, "I'm sorry I said all those things, Mr. Rightmyer. You really are a good teacher and a good poet. I embarrassed you and myself. I don't know why I acted like that."

Part of me wanted to give him the big lecture about being responsible and acting properly, but from glancing at his mother, I could tell he was going to get that talk on his ride home. He was definitely feeling bad about what happened, and instead of making him feel any worse, I put my hand on his shoulder and said, "We all make mistakes. I know you didn't mean all those things. I know you were just trying to be funny, and I appreciate your coming up to apologize."

I'll never forget the way he looked when I forgave him. All the tension and guilt seemed to leave his body. It was like he could finally breathe again. I thought he might even reach over and hug me.

"Thank you, Mr. Rightmyer," he said. "Really, I'm very sorry." The next morning when I entered school he was standing by my classroom door. He gave me an envelope and then apologized again and walked away. Inside the envelope was a note of apology. He wrote, "I thought I was being funny last night. I've learned my lesson about showing off, and I won't do it again. Thank you for understanding and accepting my apology."

I put the envelope on my desk and thought, maybe the poetry reading wasn't such a disaster after all. Quite a few of my students attended, which showed they wanted to take a risk. The parents, as usual, were helpful and supportive. One student made a mistake and acted immaturely, but he learned a lesson from it, which is one of the most important things that can happen. I also experienced, once again, that wonderful feeling of forgiving someone and giving him another chance.

Building strong RELATIONSHIPS

When I was a sophomore in college, the course I was dying to take was "Magazine Writing," taught by a long-time magazine writer who had worked at both *Time* and *Newsweek*. All summer long I kept telling my friends and relatives, "I'm taking 'Magazine Writing' this fall. It's taught by a famous journalist. Maybe after I graduate from college, I'll start working for *Time* or *Newsweek*. I might even end up living in London or Paris, and maybe I'll be a foreign correspondent." I really believed this.

"Once you have learned to love, you have learned to live."

– Unknown

That same semester, I was also taking "Introduction to German," since I had one more language class requirement. (After five years of French, I was still in the "bonjour" and "au revoir" stage.) I was not looking forward to German class. German was a language that sounded to me like speaking while you were choking on a pretzel, but with the name "Rightmyer," I figured that maybe I had some German somewhere deep in my genetic makeup.

My German teacher, Dr. Kramer, turned out to be a model of how to motivate students and how to connect individually with each of us. He was not a genuinely funny man. He was very academic, but he was relaxed enough to know when to laugh, and there was always humor in every class, usually something spontaneous. Because we felt relaxed as a group, students would often laugh about how guttural the language was or about Dr. Kramer's once-again horrible choice for a tie.

After only a week of class, he had me. I couldn't wait to get to class and speak a language that sounded like you were choking on a pretzel.

Dr. Kramer made a point of eating his bag lunch on nice days in our quad, usually surrounded by throngs of students. He got to know who we were and what we were majoring in. He was always trying to get me to read some German writers and philosophers. He would play German composers like Wagner in class, and he wasn't afraid of speaking about Nazi atrocities during World War II. By the end of that semester, I was reading German, and I wanted to take more of his German classes.

I don't even remember the name of the 'Magazine Writing' teacher. Whenever I went up to speak to him, he always seemed to be in a hurry to leave. We never laughed in his class. There wasn't any time for it. Three times a week, that class was the longest 55 minutes of my day, and I couldn't wait for it to end.

A teacher changes. Whenever I think of my friend Scott, I think of the contrast between those two teachers. Scott, a science teacher, retired a few years ago after 30 years of working with middle school students. He was part of my team of teachers back in the mid-1990's, so I saw first hand what an excellent teacher he was. He was the consummate pro, always to the school early in the morning and usually the last to leave. He prepared carefully for every class, and we always marveled at how quickly he was able to grade papers and get them back to students.

He had high expectations for both students and teachers. His students worked from the moment they entered his room until the moment they left. He had a very specific curriculum to follow, and nothing was going to get in the way. The content was what mattered most to Scott. He had no time for silly questions.

I liked him very much, even though he was the complete opposite of me. When I'd go hiking with him, he would come with maps and enough provisions for us to stay out in the wild for weeks on end. I would usually forget my water bottle. We once attended a conference about right and left brain learners. Scott clearly falls into the left brain, analytical category, and I am off the charts right brain—creative but not always sure what day of the week it is. For years after that conference, I kept asking Scott if I was right-brained or left-brained because as a typical right-brainer I was always forgetting. Scott had tremendous patience, and finally after a few years announced, "Jack, think of it this way, *Right*myer, right brain!" That worked.

As a teacher I believe in the importance of content, but I also feel that getting to know my students and creating a positive relationship with them is just as important. Scott often questioned why there was so much laughing going on in my room during class time. He was sort of old school, which meant that laughing didn't happen in the classroom. Work happened. He was used to dealing in facts, a lot of them, and maybe he thought creating a relationship with his students would only get in the way.

As a perfectionist, Scott often complained about the shoddy work of his students. "They don't know how to write," he would complain to me. "They don't know how to spell. They don't know how to study and take a test."

He also got very frustrated with the administration and many other teachers. "It's like a country club around here," he would say. "When I send a student out of my room, it's never dealt with in the office. Kids are getting away with everything!"

I knew Scott acted the way he did for all the best reasons. He really just wanted to do what was best for the kids. He really cared about them and wanted them to excel. He didn't need or want to be voted the most popular teacher.

Then Scott decided to retire. He told me at the beginning of the school year, "I've had enough. I just want to get out of here in January. It was really hard for me to come back even for this one semester."

I told him, "Well, you're going to be missed."

He laughed. "You think so. We're all easy to replace. I'll soon be forgotten."

Clearly, Scott was suffering from teacher burnout. I could sense that he still had great passion for his curriculum and the mysteries of science, but he seemed to be lacking that all-important belief that his work mattered and that he really made a difference in the lives of his students. He was suffering from a lack of positive relationships with his students.

Relationships matter. Relationships do matter, as was clearly stated in an article in an April 2005 *Middle Ground* article by well-known speaker and author, Rick Wormeli. He writes, "If we find ourselves tolerating rather than looking forward to our students, something is amiss." He subscribes to the famous adage, "Students don't care how much we know until they know how much we care."

This sounds right to me, and it describes perfectly the teachers I learned best from, teachers like Dr. Kramer. Wormeli goes on to explain that we need to cultivate healthy relationships with our students, and he explains some ways to do that:

1. We must realize that most of what happens in our classrooms and hallways isn't about us. It's about the

students. Therefore, we need to put students first, never cut them off, and always listen patiently to what they have to say.

2. We need to be purposely inviting to students and show them that we're interested in them. We do this by putting their work up around the room, standing by the door when they come into class, and always greeting them by their first name.

3. Let students know they make good company. Always ask follow-up questions about their discussions with you.

4. Convince students that we believe in them by praising them when they do something well and by applauding them when they take a risk.

5. Be well-prepared every day. This shows students that you respect them enough to present the best lessons for the topic and not just something to get through the day.

Wormeli writes, "Some teachers think that dealing with emotions in the classroom is somehow soft and takes away from their academic cause. Wrong. When there's angst in our lives, we are easily threatened by others. When we are at peace, we extend ourselves to others in a nurturing manner. There is nothing soft about cultivating good relationships with students; to avoid something so pivotal to academic success is close to malpractice."

He concludes his article with a quote from Elspeth Campbell Murphy's book, *Chalkdust.* "If I had been a kid in my class today, would I want to come back tomorrow?"

A change takes place. My friend Scott seemed to be in a relationship rut. But as the days began to creep by in September, an odd thing began to happen with Scott. He seemed happier. I saw him out in front of his room more and more, talking and laughing with students and other teachers. One day after school, I came up to him and said, "It looks like you're already counting down the days to your retirement, Scott. You seem awfully happy this year."

"It's the kids," he said. "Probably the best group I've ever had. I'm hoping that I can stay with them throughout the year. Maybe I won't retire in January after all."

Well, I thought, the kids are usually always wonderful in September, but let's see how he feels come October and those bleak barren days of November.

As the weeks rolled by, he just seemed to keep getting happier. It was like I was watching Scrooge after the ghosts had visited him. He started a science club. He looked years younger. Maybe he was finally realizing what a wonderful career teaching really is. Maybe he wasn't letting all those little things like grading, memos, faculty meetings and difficult parents get in the way of the sheer joy of teaching a subject he loved. It was energizing for me to watch this transformation from across the hall.

But in early December, he came into my room one afternoon looking very dejected. "You won't believe the way they're treating me," he said. "I wrote the administration and the superintendent a letter last week requesting that my retirement be pulled. I want to finish the year with these kids. I haven't had this much fun since I was very young."

"And they won't do that?" I asked.

"That's right," said Scott. "They've already hired a teacher to take over for me in January, and the new teacher has no experience."

I didn't know what to say. "I'm sorry," I said. "Is there anything I can do?"

"Call a school board member," he said. "You've worked with me. You know that I'm a good teacher. I've been in this school for over 20 years."

Later that day I did call a school board member. "We know Scott's an excellent teacher," she said, "but there are regulations we have to follow, and when a teacher says he's going to retire and we hire a new teacher, we can't just tell that new teacher that we don't need him anymore and unhire him. It's sad, but Scott didn't have to put his name in to retire. He can always be a substitute teacher."

When I told Scott about this, he shook his head. "That's the same thing all the other school board members are saying."

"I'm sorry," I said, "but think how lucky you are to have such a wonderful group of kids for your last few weeks."

"That's just it," said Scott, his eyes getting moist. "This is the best group I've ever had. I can't wait to get to school every day. I'm having so much fun with them every day, even though we're doing all the content. The days are just flying by, and I don't want them to fly by. Last week, for the first time ever, I was hoping that we wouldn't have a snow day because I want to be here every day. Isn't that weird?"

"That's pretty weird," I said and smiled.

"You've always been real popular with your students," said Scott, "but I've never had that, ever. A few of them were playing in a basketball game last Sunday and they invited me to go watch. No kids have ever invited me to do anything. So I went to the game, and they got so excited when I showed up. It meant so much to them. I never knew teaching could ever be this much fun, and now they all want to see me play in next week's faculty hoop game after school. I never play in those games, but I think I'm going to play this year."

Not only did Scott play in the game, but he even scored a basket. He probably had more fans than any other teacher playing, and his fans brought signs and screamed his name. He talked about it for weeks after. "I felt like a rock star," he said.

During his last week, he had kids staying after school every day helping him clean up his room, and many of them brought presents for him. The kids all seemed sad to see him go, and many parents even attended a school board meeting to ask that he remain their child's teacher.

It was an emotional day for him on that last Friday, and he was very bitter toward the administration, but he kept it together, the consummate professional right up to the last second of the last period of the day.

"I never knew I liked teaching this much," he said that last afternoon when all the kids had gone home, "and now I can't do it anymore."

I didn't know what to say. "You can always correct my papers," I said, trying to get him to smile.

"No, I'm not going to miss that. I'm going to miss the kids," he said.

I think what he had discovered in those last few weeks of his 30 year teaching career was that forming positive relationships with students really does matter. It may have taken him a long time, but like Scrooge, he finally understood what was really important.

About a month later, I got an e-mail from him. "I've been sub-bing mostly fourth and fifth grade. I love it. Most of the elementary teachers don't know a lot about science so I've been helping them and doing some workshops. I miss my kids at the middle school, but I'm happy."

I wrote back. "Scott, I'm sure those kids miss you very much. We all miss you, but how lucky you are that you've got another new group to teach. And how lucky those kids are to have you!"

SMILES on the Last Day

For over 40 years now, I've been involved with the end of a school year, either as a student or a teacher. As a student, the last day of school usually consisted of laughing, jumping up and down, and screaming. It was the day I normally ran off the school bus and all the way home in the hope of getting as much time as possible out of summer vacation.

But there were a few transition years, like eighth grade and twelfth grade, when I sort of lingered at school for a while, not quite so eager to move on to my next challenge. Those were the years when I spent a little more time than usual writing comments in my friends' yearbooks. At the end of my senior year in college, I didn't want to deal with the reality that I had graduated, which meant I could go home and start working at a real job. I even moved into a crummy apartment in the Bronx with a few of my school friends and tried to prolong, even by a month, the last of my college days.

"Be nice to people on your way up because you meet them on the way down."

– Jimmy Durante

At the end of each of my first few years as a teacher, I felt like an airline pilot who had safely crossed the Atlantic Ocean in a driving storm with only one working engine. But now I usually feel a mixture of both excitement and sadness—excitement that my daily teaching routine will be ending, and sadness that students I've grown to really enjoy are leaving.

That last day of school is also the day I say good-bye to my retiring co-workers. They always say, "I'll be back to visit next year. Maybe I'll even sub a few days." But I know they will probably not return.

A few of my favorite students usually stop in to say their farewells. I sign their yearbooks and tell them to keep in touch. Sometimes they do.

SMILES

on the Last Day

At the end of every school year, usually during the last week, there's at least one moment that reminds me that teaching is such a great job. One year it was my Chinese student Jian Hai, the boy who couldn't speak English, who said to me slowly and through a smile, "Thank you. You good teacher."

Another year it was Sean, a boy who was always getting into some kind of mischief throughout the year because he was so hyper and had a habit of screaming things out during class and falling out of his chair. He's the kind of kid that most teachers don't mind saying goodbye to. But there was something about him that I found appealing. Maybe it was his small size that reminded me so much of myself when I was his age, and maybe it was that he never did anything that was malicious. He just seemed to have a difficult time controlling all that energy he had stored up in his little body.

At least once a week I had to keep Sean after class and talk to him about some inappropriate behavior. Sean was always apologetic, and he usually assured me that he'd do better next time, and sometimes he would do better.

And on the last day of school, there he was with a grin that stretched across his face. Most students were moving quickly through the hallway to get outside and onto the bus and escape to their freedom, but Sean handed me an envelope and said, "Read this when I'm gone." Then he raced out the door and into the crowded hallway.

"Bye, Sean," I yelled after him. "Have a good summer. Keep in touch." But I don't think he heard any of this. I opened the envelope and found a poem that he had copied down for me.

My Friend

You are but one small voice I'll hear in my life
So are the thoughts you helped me with
For this I say thank you to my Teacher
My Friend, and hope the time will be short
Between when I see you again

I stood there alone in my classroom and once again realized what a wonderful job teaching is. From September through June, teachers are in that classroom struggling to make some difference in the lives of kids. We hope that students are learning a few valuable skills that might one day come in handy when they're out of school and working. Maybe they'll even gain some positive values that might help them become better people. We are not always sure if we have reached a student, but sometimes the revelation hits and all that preparation, all that time, all that paper correcting seems worth it, and we are so happy to have chosen education as a career. And many times, just when we begin to see some improvement in our hardest to reach kids, it's time to say good-bye.

Not wanting to say good-bye. About 15 years ago, we had an exceptional group of students at the middle school where I now teach, and we just didn't want to say good-bye. We wanted to keep teaching them as they moved on to eighth grade, then high school and even on to college. We all stood there, all five of us who had taught this amazing group day after day, and we watched them race through the hallways to their buses. Our classrooms felt so empty already, and more than a few of us were actually tearing up.

"Let's go out to the buses and wave good-bye to them," said one of my teacher friends.

We all agreed that it was a great idea, so that's what we did. As we walked through the hall, we told other teachers, "Come on. Let's go wave good-bye to the kids."

Other teachers joined us, and when we got to the parking lot, there were over 15 of us waving to the buses as they drove by and blowing kisses to the kids. The kids were laughing and waving back. Some of the bus drivers were shaking their heads at the crazy teachers, and a few of them were waving to us and honking their horns. Kids began pressing handmade signs on bus windows:

"We love you."

"Have a great summer."

"See you next year!"

That "good-bye" has now become a tradition. It has grown through the years, and today we have over 100 teachers who make the annual trek to wave good-bye in the parking lot.

The last image our students have is a group of teachers arm-in-arm, kicking up their legs, singing, waving and most definitely showing their love to the students as they are bused away. Some of us have a few tears, but all of us are smiling and laughing, and I can't think of a better way to end our school year.

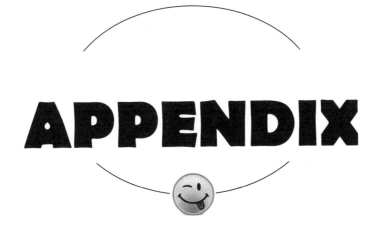

APPENDIX

A Unit on **HUMOR**

When I was a high school teacher, my students mostly hung in there during the last weeks of school because they had a final they needed to pass. We did review for the last few weeks, boring but practical stuff, and students jumped through the hoops and, for the most part, finished up the year rather passively. They did what I asked, studied for the final, and we parted ways mostly on amicable terms.

But then I began teaching at the middle school. My sixth and seventh graders didn't have to take a final at the end of the year. For that last week, I used to feel like a babysitter.

Many people would sooner die than think. In fact they do.
—Bertrand Russel

I needed to come up with something that would keep students' attention during the last few weeks of school. I needed something that was academic, high interest and hopefully fun and creative at the same time. I don't know when the idea came to me, but when it did, I knew I had found my missing three-week unit. I would teach a unit on humor at the end of the year.

For quite a few years, I had begun to experiment more and more with using humor in my classroom, trying out a funny poem, a funny essay or story, or a funny recording or humorous tape from a TV show or movie. Whenever I did this, my classes always perked up. That had a profound impact on my teaching since the more interested my students became, the more energized I became.

My humor unit has evolved through the years, and it changes somewhat every year. What follows is a description of a typical unit for my sixth and seventh grade classes.

Day 1. I begin the unit by having my students take 5-10 minutes to write about a funny event or story that may have happened to them or to someone they know. They don't need to supply names, and if it was something embarrassing that happened to them, they can certainly say it happened to someone they know.

After they write the story in their classroom journals, we take some time for them to share what they've written. I always make a point of sharing my journal, too. (By this time of the school year, my students are usually very comfortable in sharing what they've written).

With 10-15 minutes to go in class, I stop calling on students for their responses and inform them that we are going to begin a unit on humor. We discuss the following questions:

- Why is humor good for your health?
- Is there any type of humor that can be harmful?

Day 2. I begin the class by bringing in some of my favorite books of humor by some of the following authors: David Sedaris, Mark Twain, Jean Shepherd, Paula Danziger, Dave Barry, and Gordon Korman.

I read a few excerpts, hoping to excite my students about reading humor. I ask about humorous books they have read, and I write some of their titles and favorite authors on the board. We then go to our media center, where the librarian does a brief presentation on books of humor. Then students have 10-15 minutes to select a book from the humor section. When I bring the students back to my room, I explain that they should read at least 15 pages a day. If there is time, we all begin reading quietly in class.

Day 3. I ask students if they are enjoying the books they're reading. Have they found any funny passages yet? Would they like to read those funny passages?

I then define, with the help of the class, the four different types of humor that will be the focus of our humor unit: *parody, satire, farce* and *irony*. The students get into groups of two or three to come up with examples of the different types of humor.

Day 4: I ask the class if they have ever seen the movie A *Christmas Story*. Then I show a five-minute clip from the film and afterwards talk briefly about the author of the story, Jean Shepherd, who often wrote about his childhood and used a lot of exaggeration as the basis for his humor. I ask the class, "Can you think of any other movies, TV shows or books that also use exaggeration as a basis for humor?"

Then, as a class, we read aloud "Lost At C," a story by Jean Shepherd. When we're done reading, we usually have about 5-10 minutes left, and I have students get together in groups and find examples of exaggeration in the story.

Day 5. We review what *parody* means. I show a five-minute clip of some *Saturday Night Live* parodies of commercials. We discuss other types of parodies students have seen or read. I have students break up into groups of three or four to prepare a brief parody based on either a commercial, TV show, movie, book, fairy tale, or something else of their own choice. I give them the rest of the class to prepare and practice.

Day 6: Students take half the class and act out their parody skits. I then ask the students if they are reading any examples of parody in their books of humor. For the last 5-10 minutes, I ask for volunteers to come forward and "become" a character in the book they are reading and discuss what is happening to them. If there is time, each volunteer conducts a press conference as his or her character. The class asks the questions.

Day 7: We review what *satire* means. I show a video clip of satire from a Saturday Night Live episode or an old Monty Python movie. We brainstorm some problems happening in our world today—poverty, pollution, war, etc. We then discuss how writers could use satire to make a point about these problems. I give students 10-15 minutes to begin a satire (essay, editorial cartoon, story, poem, etc). With 5-10 minutes to go I ask for any student volunteers to read aloud what they have written.

Day 8: We review what *farce* means. I show a 5-10 minute video clip of an example of farce (Woody Allen movie, Monty Python movie, *Saturday Night Live*, etc.) I take some time to talk about the book *The Secret Diary of Adrian Mole, Aged 13 3/4*. I point out that a diary entry can be a great way to create farce. We brainstorm some possible funny diaries (Noah, Noah's wife, diary of a dog, diary of a mannequin, etc). I give students 5-10 minutes to create a funny diary entry. For the last 5-10 minutes, I encourage students to read aloud their diary entries.

Day 9: We review what *irony* means. We read aloud some funny accident reports that people have written and some funny mistakes that have been found in church bulletins. I have the students get together in pairs to talk about times in their lives when something ironic happened to them or when they saw something ironic happen to another person. Then I pass out an essay I published, loaded with irony, about my daughter's first birthday party. I explain how I wrote the article, and we discuss the examples of irony in the piece.

Day 10: Students take 15-20 minutes and write about the book of humor they are reading. They provide examples of parody, satire, farce and/or irony from the book. After handing in their writing, students then read quietly from their books. If a student has already finished his book, I provide a funny essay or story for him to read.

Day 11: We begin working on our end-of-the-unit humor project, which will be a classroom book of humor. The students break into five groups: layout department, parody department, satire department, farce department and irony department. Students may work together to write poetry, an essay, a story or create a cartoon. Each category must be represented in the book of humor, and the book must be completed on the third day. Stories and essays should not be longer than one page.

Days 12, 13 and 14: Students report to the computer room in the media center and work on their classroom book of humor. On the third day, the book needs to be completed.

Day 15: We share the finished book of humor and discuss how the project went. Was the book completed on time? Did the class work well together?

I have had many variations of this three-week humor unit, but I have always found that it is a great way to keep my students focused and working hard in those last tedious and muggy days of school. My students learn that it takes some work to be funny. It's not as easy as most comedians make it look. They also learn that humor, when done right, can be a way to bring about some change in our society and in the way we all live.

It's also just a fun way to finish up the school year.

About the **AUTHOR**

Jack Rightmyer is a seventh grade English teacher at Bethlehem Central Middle School in Delmar, New York. He is also an adjunct professor at Siena College and a book reviewer at the *Daily Gazette* in Schenectady, New York.

"Life is too important to be taken seriously."

— Oscar Wilde

For more resources on humor, the author recommends:

The HUMOR Project
480 Broadway, Suite 210
Saratoga Springs, New York 12866-2288

www.humorproject.com

MORE GREAT BOOKS FROM COTTONWOOD PRESS

A SENTENCE A DAY—Short, playful proofreading exercises to help students avoid tripping up when they write. This book focuses on short, playful, interesting sentences with a sense of humor.

DOWNWRITE FUNNY—Using student's love of the ridiculous to build serious writing skills. The entertaining activities and illustrations in this book help teach all kinds of useful writing skills.

HOT FUDGE MONDAY—Tasty Ways to Teach Parts of Speech to Students Who Have a Hard Time Swallowing Anything To Do With Grammar. This new edition includes quirky quizzes, extended writing activities, and Internet enrichment activities that reinforce new skills.

HOW TO HANDLE DIFFICULT PARENTS—A teacher's survival guide. Suzanne Capek Tingley identifies characteristics of some parent "types". She then goes on to give practical, easy-to-implement methods of working with them more effectively.

IF THEY'RE LAUGHING THEY JUST MIGHT BE LISTENING—Ideas for using HUMOR effectively in the classroom—even if you're NOT funny yourself. Discover ways to lighten up, encourage humor from others, and have fun with your students.

LANGUAGE IS SERVED—An activity book that encourages students to have fun with language. Fun activities loosely centered on a theme of interest to all—food. The author uses a light touch and her trademark sense of humor to teach difficult subjects.

PHUNNY STUPH—Your students will smile and sharpen their proofreading skills as they correct the jokes and urban legends. The activities contain just about every error you can imagine, from spelling and punctuation mistakes to sentence fragments and run-ons.

RELUCTANT DISCIPLINARIAN—Advice on classroom management from a softy who became (eventually) a successful teacher. Author Gary Rubinstein offers clear and specific advice for classroom management.

THINKING IN THREES—The Power of Three in Writing. Faced with a writing task of any kind? Think of three things to say about the topic. Writing an essay? Remember that the body should have at least three paragraphs. Need help getting started? Learn three ways to begin an essay.

TWISTING ARMS—Teaching students how to write to persuade. This book is full of easy-to-use activities that will really sharpen students' writing and organizational skills.

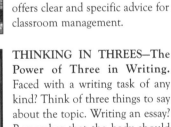

COTTONWOOD PRESS INC.
www.cottonwoodpress.com